LEAN HUMAN RESOURCES

Redesigning HR Processes for a Culture of Continuous Improvement

LEAN HUMAN RESOURCES

Redesigning HR Processes for a Culture of Continuous Improvement

Cheryl M. Jekiel

CRC Press
Taylor & Francis Group
Boca Raton   London   New York

CRC Press is an imprint of the
Taylor & Francis Group, an **informa** business

A PRODUCTIVITY PRESS BOOK

Productivity Press
Taylor & Francis Group
270 Madison Avenue
New York, NY 10016

© 2011 by Taylor and Francis Group, LLC
Productivity Press is an imprint of Taylor & Francis Group, an Informa business

No claim to original U.S. Government works

Printed in the United States of America on acid-free paper
10 9 8 7 6 5 4 3 2 1

International Standard Book Number: 978-1-4398-1306-5 (Paperback)

Library of Congress Cataloging-in-Publication Data

Jekiel, Cheryl M.
    Lean human resources : redesigning HR processes for a culture of continuous improvement / Cheryl M. Jekiel.
        p. cm.
    Includes index.
    ISBN 978-1-4398-1306-5 (pbk. : alk. paper)
    1. Personnel management. 2. Quality control--Management. 3. Organizational effectiveness. I. Title.

HF5549.J457 2011
658.3'01--dc22
                                                       2010026550

Visit the Taylor & Francis Web site at
http://www.taylorandfrancis.com

and the Productivity Press Web site at
http://www.productivitypress.com

Contents

SECTION V STRATEGIES FOR ALIGNING YOUR HR PROCESSES

Acknowledgments

Thanks to Jean Cunningham for the encouragement to get started.

Thanks to Fred, Bob, John, and many others who have shared their experiences with me and led me to see the ways that Lean and HR truly connect.

Thanks to Mary Pat, Amy, Ruth, Peggy, and Bill, who made writing this book a great learning experience.

Ted – You are my best friend and your love and support always cheer me on.

Introduction

At one level, this book is a methodology for companies to involve the Human Resources department in attaining improved business results by providing necessary support to the required cultural transformations. Yet the more important issue with why HR is often absent from business improvement efforts is the mostly massive waste of people's talents inside the workplace. Optimizing more of your people's abilities remains one of the largest opportunities to achieve better profitability, quality, and service levels, which may be critical to your organization's survival in our current global economy.

Of course, this idea is hardly new. Efforts over several decades to develop people's contributions in their work have been a key component of Process Improvement, Continuous Improvement, or Lean Implementations. Yet why have many of these efforts been deemed unsuccessful? Often because the cultural change required eludes most who attempt the challenge, which is where the issue comes full circle. *Organizations are wasting significant amounts of their people's talent to transform work cultures, but their efforts, which would work to more fully utilize people, often fail. These significant business problems are amplified by weaknesses in how the HR department is utilized. In addition, the failure to more fully involve HR and all related HR systems and programs are key reasons for unsuccessful Lean implementations or business improvement efforts.*

Who This Book Can Help

Although the book assumes the reader knows about Continuous Improvement or Lean Implementations, it can be of great help to any reader who wants to better understand how strengthening the HR department can help optimize the application of people's abilities in the workplace.

Human resources executives and professionals: Many HR professionals working in organizations that are pursuing Continuous Improvement or Lean Cultures will benefit from getting a game plan for the role of HR in Lean Implementations. However, HR professionals working in any organization that is ready to have HR be better business partners would be well served by many of the concepts laid out in the material and the strengthening of HR as a business partner.

Business owners, CEOs, or general managers: This book is also for those who want to create an improved vision of the role of the HR professional. CEOs of organizations pursuing Lean or Continuous Improvement initiatives will find this book helpful in knowing what to have HR contribute to the effort, as well as more about what it takes to create a Continuous Improvement culture.

Operations executives and managers: Operations is continually seeking improved results, whether or not as formally part of Process Improvement or Lean Implementations. Yet these professionals need to raise their expectations of what to seek from their HR professionals to create a function that provides the value needed to achieve their objectives. The time has come for Operations to insist HR be fully part of the charge toward progress.

Lean practitioners: Working full time to improve functions is the task of some professionals in an external or internal consulting roles. I have found many of these individuals to be quite knowledgeable about the potential role of HR, but they are frustrated by the fact that HR is often not included in improvement activities. This book may provide more insight into how to seek HR involvement as well as insights as to what might be in the way. Most important, the book lays out the real risk of leaving HR out of the process.

Why You Should Read This Book Now

A pivotal conversation that convinced me to spend a year writing this book was with a major company that is well known as a leader in driving a quality culture and devoted to Lean principles. This organization widely speaks to other companies that the path to success lies in a culture of "Lean principles." In this conversation, I happened to be talking to two top leaders in the operations area and asked, "What role does HR have in your initiatives or the advancement of the culture?" To my amazement, they both looked at each other as though I had asked an odd question. They almost simultaneously said with a shrug that HR was more part of the problem their group was trying to get around. It was then that I decided I had heard that answer too many times, and if the answer was so commonly understood among leading-edge companies that the HR group is "part of the problem," then it was time for me to make HR's role clearer.

I've been fortunate to be able to work with and observe so many companies that are thinking in new ways about how to tap into the talents of their people, how to engage their people more, and how to have their people work better at solving problems and utilize their judgment in ways that have never before been seen. Yet the fact that HR still lags behind in its role in leading this cause drives me to want to educate organizations on increasing the expectations of HR.

When the HR department is in the background, cultural change or the optimization of people cannot be possible. This book begins with coming to understand why the HR department is often the weakest group within an organization, and then it provides a range of approaches to strengthening the HR department. These changes then allow for complete cultural transformations as well as the optimization of the talents in the workforce, referred to here as Lean Human Resources.

Lean Human Resources, as a set of strategic solutions, can help you strengthen the role of your HR department, to support a strong work culture and improved HR processes, which can thereby reduce the waste of your people's abilities—and improve your company's financial results as well as your customers' satisfaction. Once the HR department possesses clarity about its role and the skills to fulfill that role, it will be able to effectively implement and maintain work cultures that meet strategic objectives. A stronger HR department is also then able to redesign basic work programs and practices that develop the abilities of people and how those contributions are brought to bear in the workplace.

A Background in Business, Lean, and HR

My knowledge that human resources was the field of dreams for me started at age 16, when I bought my first car from someone who owned a firm specializing in career development. I was completely intrigued by a profession devoted to the link between psychology and business. It took a few jobs for me to get there, beginning as a retirement plans analyst, which led to being a pension consultant, which finally allowed me to move into a real HR department as the retirement plans manager.

Fortunately, my first real HR position was within an organization that launched a Process Improvement Program that provided my first lessons in zero defects and waste removal, which changed my perspective on life and work forever. When a mistake was made, my manager kept asking me, "How are you going to make sure this doesn't happen again?" At first, the question seemed cruel and heartless. Then the light went on: my manager wasn't trying to rub my nose in the mistake, but to get me to really consider what would have to change to prevent that mistake from ever being repeated. Now that was a challenge worth pursuing.

The next big lesson in waste removal involved figuring out that an entire position in my department was unnecessary when we examined each step of the work and found out every paper being filed had a duplicate in another location. We also seldom pulled these records, so why would we need a full-time person putting it all away? My view of work has been suspect ever since about whether people potentially devote their time and effort to work that isn't necessary. These early lessons propelled me to seek leadership roles in Process Improvement.

Yet I was almost immediately frustrated with the role of HR in the improvement efforts. It was less a matter of how the organization viewed HR, but that the HR function was not at the strategy table, and was a minimal part of the improvement effort. I couldn't understand how someone would not see how critical HR would be to achieving results over time. Why did the person in charge of the department devoted to *people* not see how to really add the value that was potentially there?

Over the next 15 years, I learned an amazing amount about processes, expanding job roles, teamwork, waste removal, and eliminating defects. Using benchmarking and some outside help, we implemented a skill plan that produced more good product with many fewer people because of cross training and broader skill ranges. These new jobs required team skills and the knowledge of how to apply product quality standards. Up until then, managers just accepted that some employees had terrible attitudes and didn't want to try or get along with others. I also learned about change agents who were brave enough to be very different than other managers—even if they were alone.

What makes my career path unusual is that I went from an HR role into general management as chief operating officer of a mid-size company. My career progressed this way due to implementing Lean programs as key elements of my role as the head of Human Resources. HR people rarely go into general management, because their business skills are not strong enough and they don't contribute sufficiently to the organization.

During those years, I joined the Association of Manufacturing Excellence, which is a network of organizations that share best practices in large part through tours and workshops in member facilities. Much of what I've learned about what is possible in organizations has come from visiting other organizations and learning what works in other situations. Many of the industries would be vastly different from mine, but the lessons in how to tap into the talents of people would all transfer directly.

Along the way, I developed a new vision for HR that was profoundly affected by two principles. First, that HR as a support function tends to be dead weight on the bottom line. Second, HR needs to add value in a manner that could be considered valuable enough that internal customers would pay for the service if necessary.

The idea of support functions as dead weight came from World-Class Manufacturing that laid out a business as functions that either made product or sold product. All other expenses had to be minimized because they did neither. Therefore, the staff expenses under the most scrutiny were the support functions, like finance and human resources. These departments had to be transformed to add more value to the business because they didn't actually make or sell product.

In addition to the idea that HR had to work against being "dead weight" on the system, I set about understanding how HR needed to raise the bar set by its customers (the employees) to have a real sense of value. HR also needed to evolve to better help increase revenue or decrease costs. It was obvious then, and it is still equally true now.

How This Book Is Organized

This book is divided into four sections, which work together to lay the groundwork for people-related programs, policies, and practices that allow people to achieve more. At the heart of this work is coming to a deeper understanding of how workplaces restrict real people's potential and how to develop strategies for unleashing their actual capabilities in the workplace.

Section I reviews ways organizations waste the abilities of people on a massive scale. Chapter 1 begins with highlighting how the waste of people's abilities is largely unseen and represents a tremendous opportunity to improve all aspects of key results. Chapter 2 presents a clear review of how Lean efforts require cultural change and how the absence of HR has been partly to blame for many improvement efforts failing, as well as what would be the value of having HR fully involved in improvement projects.

Section II provides a vision for a new HR department that can be a business partner and create unsurpassed customer service levels for employees, and describes the skills needed to accomplish these tasks. Chapter 3 focuses on why HR has been in the background of improvement efforts due to difficulties in evolving beyond historical administrative, union relations, and policing roles. Chapter 4 presents a new vision for HR in the workplace as a business partner. Chapter 5 provides a look at how to apply Lean methods to HR processes to help build skills and, more important, to streamline HR work to allow for more time and resources for business partnering. Chapter 6 reviews how HR can help companies better implement business strategies and corresponding people-related strategies and cultures. This chapter compares traditional business strategies to those of organizations pursuing Lean principles as they now have a natural bias toward recognizing the strength of people's talents and abilities that need to be supported (if not championed) by HR.

Section III begins with understanding how the power of people, processes, and participation can drive the achievement of the business strategy. The need to achieve a strategy by impacting people's behavior is covered in terms of work culture in this section, which involves values, policies, practices, and attitudes. Chapter 7 provides an initial overview that defines "culture" and the characteristics of Lean cultures that are often pursued by organizations that seek better ways to operate. Chapter 8 provides clear methods for HR to support the implementation of cultures that support improved business results. Chapter 9 looks for various aspects of the workplace that support, detract from, or are neutral toward desired cultural characteristics to highlight the importance of ensuring alignment for successful cultures. Chapter 10 provides methods for measuring progress, including employee, customer, and culture surveys.

Section IV provides a roadmap for how traditional HR programs can be redesigned to provide more value. Beginning with job roles, Chapter 11 provides a methodology for enlarging jobs to better access people's potential by building improvement-linked competencies or skills into each job. Chapter 12 provides a basis for documenting jobs, which in turn provides a standard work format for a wide range of managerial roles, as well as other positions. Section V provides strategies for aligning HR processes. After jobs are designed and documented from Section IV, Chapter 13 pulls through the design into basic HR programs in terms of how they need to be redesigned to optimize people's abilities. Chapter 14 provides a 5-year plan for implementing strategies, as described in Chapter 13, to ensure changes are well planned, paced correctly and effectively put into operation.

Section VI is designed especially for CEOs. One of the key ideas in Lean HR is that the weaknesses in the function are caused not only by how the HR professionals see themselves, but also how management sees the HR function. Therefore, this final section is directed at the role of the CEO in creating some of the changes needed in the workplace. Chapter 15 envisions how Lean HR strategies and methods create a highly motivating place to work. A highly motivated team of people is surely capable of more than teams of people who are merely putting in their time. So if an organization is just punching the clock or getting by, these concepts could uncover the potential of the human spirit and how to allow people's abilities to continually expand to everyone's benefit.

Using This Book

This material provides a range of strategies, methods, and techniques for improving the contribution of Human Resources, the implementation of an effective work culture, and the redesign of basic HR processes and programs. To provide guidance on implementing these ideas, each chapter contains a summary page, which highlights the principles of the chapter in key ideas, strategic questions, and specific actions:

- The highlights are a brief recap of the concepts to strengthen understanding.
- The strategic questions provide material for consideration and/or discussion to develop appropriate next steps.
- The action steps have been developed to guide efforts for moving forward with that chapter's concepts.

I've written this book as a way to really understand the multitude of ways HR is a necessary component of Lean implementations or business improvement. My hope is that you will see not only the missed opportunity from underutilizing the HR function but that you will also come to a fuller realization of how we waste people's talents and hear the call to action to make real changes so that more of people's abilities are put to use in their normal jobs. As you prepare to read this book, ask yourself the following question:

> How would your results change if you tapped into the talents of your workforce by making Human Resources one of the most effective groups in your organization?

THE PROBLEM: TOO MANY COMPANIES DON'T REALIZE THEY WASTE PEOPLE'S ABILITIES

Companies unwittingly waste much of their peoples' abilities in typical work roles. Chapter 1 outlines five hidden causes that drive this phenomenon and how recognizing this waste can be one of the greatest opportunities for organizations to improve performance.

The other significant issue that many organizations face is how improvement efforts show that cultural change is the only real answer to creating a capacity for sustained improvements. Chapter 2 will outline the reasons for these failed culture change efforts, whether they are real or imagined.

These two concerns are intimately linked in that a critical goal of the culture change for enduring improvement needs to be the optimization of people and that will require a fearless and thorough look at why an organization might have been invested in wasting talent. This challenging assessment of why so much of people's capabilities are left untapped, and the changes that must be implemented to alter this dynamic, surely leads the way to much greater success.

The failure to create strong, strategic HR departments helps ensure that the traditional modes of working with people remain intact and that a total culture change can't be completed without the full support and participation of a strong HR group. Attempting to make true cultural change must involve HR—and my experience shows that most do not. Therefore, Lean HR is focused on making the changes that need to be made while strengthening the HR department. This will ensure that people are better optimized and cultural changes are successful, which will be reviewed in Section II.

Chapter 1

Wasting Employee Talent

How is your organization coping with economic downturns? Have your customers changed the rules or their expectations? Is your organization looking for new ways to accomplish more with fewer resources? With all these challenges, how does your organization view the capabilities of your employees? Does it see the waste of people's abilities as part of the solution? Not likely. Yet limited work roles leave problems unsolved. Not demanding that people fully explore mistakes allows them to continue. If people are mostly conducting business as usual, improvements will be limited. New strategies are hindered by misaligned efforts. A small portion of people are engaged to drive success. So why then do workplaces waste talent and ability to such a large degree?

In many organizations, the typical work roles are still relatively narrow in scope and focus on precise *tasks* instead of what people *could* contribute. In addition, leadership structures are designed to keep power and authority to a few, with everyone else having little of either. Beyond the mindsets of leadership, processes need to be created to channel more of what people can deliver in a work day.

Lean principles provide a structure that appreciates the types of abilities that are commonly wasted, while also providing many of the processes that direct these abilities. Yet many of the Lean efforts have had limited success, in part because they lack the reinforcement of highly developed HR departments. Several forces have led to a great opportunity being ignored by the majority of organizations; this chapter takes a look at the root of the problem.

The Root of the Problem: Why Don't We See the Waste of Talent?

If the waste of people's abilities largely goes unnoticed, it's important to look at how this dynamic functions in terms of the underlying causes of this problem.

Hidden Cause Number 1: Work Roles Limit People by Design; Most People Can Do So Much More!

Most job roles are based on the completion of tasks as the basis for the position. For example, a common work role would be "production worker" or "driver," as defined by what the worker produces or does. The product made by a worker may need to meet required quality standards, or be carried out within a required time frame, but the focus is on a relatively small number of tasks. Yet these same "production workers" or "drivers" *are capable of so much more,* as demonstrated by their involvement in a variety of complex issues outside the workplace—such as raising families, running households, managing their own businesses, and other activities that validate the variety of talents within the workforce.

Organizations put people into cross-functional problem-solving teams and find many employees possess tremendous leadership skills that have gone unnoticed when they spend their day making product or handling goods with little interaction. It's not just a matter of rare abilities that could be uncovered, but that a significant number of people can lead, make decisions, generate ideas, and perform other valuable tasks, all of which tends to go unnoticed in narrow work roles. Other people are good at other types of work that go unnoticed as well, if it's not in their work role. For example, one work team had someone who had been handling a fairly simple piece of equipment as part of his daily job. Yet this team found this person was quite able to also fabricate steel, weld, and design a piece of equipment to handle an improved work design for an area.

The spirit of Lean is based on the vision that each worker is greater than the sum of his or her tasks and is capable of solving systemic problems of the organization, generating improved methods of operating, and working with other people in ways that generate better results over time.

Hidden Cause Number 2: Power Is Limited to Only a Few People

The comfort of assigning power to a few is deeply ingrained and restricts much of the talent or abilities that could make a significant difference. With so much wasted ability, it becomes obvious that this situation provides some benefit to those in leadership roles. Why? Managers often believe they are in leadership roles because they think better, solve problems better, and generally have more ability than those they lead. Managers have not been encouraged to demonstrate that the people they manage are at least as or more capable than themselves. Managers actually often see the need to maintain their roles as vested in proving no one below them can compare to their abilities.

For example, the other day I was talking to a manager about how he was managing his team, and he casually noted that it was important that he consistently demonstrate the reason he was in charge was because he knew the most about how to make the product as well as the best ways to resolve problems. It struck me that the belief that "a manager's position is based on being the best at the work" is quite common and held with deep conviction, which keeps managers motivated to ensure their team members do not outperform them in any way. Having organizational structures that are based on proving the manager is the most competent maintains the paradigms that keep power and authority restricted to a few.

Hidden Cause Number 3: People Are Reluctant to Do More Work

A familiar response from management to the question of why people do not participate more fully is "people do not want to do any more than they are paid for in their jobs." A prevalent assumption exists that people *could* do more, but they don't *want* to do more. In fairness, some of this is true: for example, I was working with a team leader recently who mentioned her frustration in dealing with a team member who had commented during a meeting: "I'm just here to do my job. Nothing else. Don't ask me for ideas. I don't want to be on any teams." This team leader was frustrated at this attitude and exclaimed that these comments just don't make sense.

My concern for this team leader is that she would take the comment of one individual as proof of anything about her team as a whole. It can be easy to take this negative comment and make it a deterrent to moving the team's skills forward. Don't let the voice of one person overly affect the team as a whole. These same "problem team members" have often proven later to be valuable assets, once they see that improvements might make their life easier (and not a matter of working more).

Also, when the cause of people's reluctance is examined, a range of concerns often arises. Many people have historically been asked to "just do your job" and not to think or interact with others while they are working. Because changes are unsettling for anyone, this means changes in working conditions can be difficult, but not insurmountable.

People are generally afraid of doing something new often because they are afraid of failing. Others may complain about not doing more because they worry they won't be able to make a difference or because they're not aware of what they might gain if they did come out of their shells. Although all these attitudes present challenges in how to shift people into a fresh outlook, they are not impossible.

Hidden Cause Number 4: Channeling Abilities Creates New Work

Beyond problems with common *attitudes*, many workplaces lack the *processes* needed to manage the output of people's abilities. The problem with allowing people to contribute more is that those activities create more activities and even more activities.

For example, if people participate in identifying problems, more problems are surfaced each day. These problems generate more ideas and possible changes to consider. In turn, these changes create even more possible solutions to evaluate. Then these solutions turn into plans that need to be developed and implemented, which initiates even more work to ensure actions are prioritized and well executed. Because fully allowing people to express their talents presents so much work, it begins to form another reason for why management allows so much talent to lay dormant.

For example, during my first experience with creating multiple improvement teams, we quickly found that the teams created sizable lists of items to research, purchase, and implement. These same teams also created the need for procedures to be developed, which then had to be written, communicated, and followed up on. It did not take more than a matter of weeks for the supervisors and managers to feel they were dropping the ball by not being able to keep up with the additional work load. The first solution proposed was to stop having the teams meet—to bring the work load back down. This seemed incredulous to me, because the lists seemed to have worthwhile activities. The real issue was in being able to generate new avenues of implementing solutions, which would not bottleneck at a few managers.

Hidden Cause Number 5: There's No Assigned Cost to People Working at Lower Capacity

The massive waste of people's abilities means that most organizations achieve only a fraction of what they could accomplish. Many establishments need to produce more efficiently than they currently do, and with less expense. For many organizations, a change in methods is needed to realize their missions. The cost of not meeting commitments can lead to the loss of jobs, revenues, customers, or even the demise of the organization itself. Understanding how to access people's abilities eludes organizations, or they surely would better utilize people to resolve troubling problems or create the needed solutions.

The acceptance of this situation is notably reflected in the lack of any reference to or concern about the unused capacity of the workforce. Most assets of a business are assessed in terms of capacity, such as buildings or equipment utilization. However, management teams rarely discuss the percentage of people's abilities being utilized each day. However, seeing the available *capacity in the workforce* is an essential element of Lean or Continuous Improvement cultures.

An early example of using job redesign for productivity occurred at a local major company that had doubled its revenue while simultaneously reducing its workforce by half, by expanding people's roles. This organization presented to several HR audiences the design of a skill plan that had people train in more areas so they could cover more jobs, which greatly reduced the number of individuals needed in the facility. The workers were able to earn more money by having a wide variety of skills, which was highly motivational for them as well.

The Solution: Seven Lean Principles Uncover People's True Capabilities

The foundation of Lean brings to light the gifts and talents of each person to a great extent. Traditional workplaces fail to ignite people's passion. If workplaces could channel more of people's passion, what would be gained? People would be more focused, interested, and able to achieve goals. Lean principles focus on people's abilities with customers, improvement, involvement, processes, problem solving, measurements, and leadership, as shown in the following list of common wastes of people's ability to

1. Keep the customer in mind (or purpose)
2. Learn from mistakes and improve
3. Generate ideas and identify concerns
4. Understand the entire process (and change when needed)
5. Solve problems with wisdom, judgment, and creativity
6. Work against goals that are visibly measured
7. Demonstrate personal leadership

Let's take a closer look at each of these capabilities.

Capability Number 1: Keeping Customers (and the Company's Purpose) in Mind

The failure to have workers focus on the customers they serve wastes their ability to work with *purpose*. In contrast, continuous improvement cultures characteristically begin with the customer in mind.

For example, in the first organization in which I worked on continuous improvement, we made the customers more real to our employees. A wide range of training sessions explained who the customers were, their concerns, and what our customers were struggling to accomplish in the marketplace. We began to have the logos of customers commonly reflected on our bulletin boards and even had customer representatives come in to speak with our people. Over time, people spoke of the importance of problems in the bigger pictures. People were *energized* by understanding the bigger picture and seeing our customers as people with concerns—not just an abstract concept.

This showed me how people initially saw their work as just a job, as in "I make plates" or "I make straws," compared to *"I make straws for a well-known restaurant chain that needs our best efforts to be successful."* As the workers in this organization saw the customers as people they had met and come to know, their attitudes changed. People would come forward with ideas that seemed urgent to them as they joined the causes of our customers. It gave them a greater sense of purpose and direction. Generally, people work better with a sense of purpose, which in turn improves their decision making and customer-related communications.

Ordinary jobs rarely require customer awareness or knowledge. Even managers are often not required to know much about customers internally or externally. A type of arrogance reigns, which seems to say, "people don't really need to understand much—they just need to do their jobs." Along with this attitude, typical HR roles have not included developing approaches to help employees better understand customers or what they need.

Capability Number 2: Learning to Improve

Lean cultures, by definition, are devoted to continuous improvement, which inherently requires people to actively learn. The ability to learn exists in several ways, including:

■ From experience
■ From how others have failed or succeeded
■ By looking underneath the surface of a situation to uncover the hidden causes

Again, many jobs don't require people to learn. Managers seem content with the idea that only *they* themselves must learn on a daily basis. Common attitudes about large groups of people include that they do not need to learn, they are not capable of learning, and they could not contribute anything important if they did learn. These attitudes artificially limit people from exploring what they could contribute by learning in a variety of ways during the work day. These attitudes also contribute to HR not having any clear role in supporting learning processes in the workplace.

For example, I was actively involved for a number of years in an organization referred to as "Learning Organizations." It took awhile to comprehend what it meant to actively promote learning in an organization and why that would be a clear benefit. I saw many large well-known organizations participate and share how they were transforming their organizations by promoting learning in their ranks.

One particular organization described the benefit as the power of a stealth jet. It would be very quiet at first, but once you got the feel of the power involved, there was nothing like it. This organization had developed the ability to quickly learn from its key statistics and make changes more proactively than reactively. This organization's leaders had originally reviewed the results at the end of the quarter and often focused on who to rake over the coals for poor results. In contrast, they became a learning organization and began to look at things monthly and even weekly, with an eye on what to change to get better results, not just who was going to get raked over the coals.

Another organization began to teach others how to look forward and develop plans for a range of possible situations to get ahead of problems. These were all lessons in how to make learning a skill, with processes that actively support this avenue to generate better results.

Capability Number 3: Generating Ideas

Lean cultures are founded on the idea that all the people in the organization need to participate by sharing ideas, concerns, and thoughts in order to create a better result. People are capable of contributing a wide range of ideas, suggestions, identified opportunities, concerns, observations, etc.

I've seen people suggest how to better store equipment so that it can be found when needed. I've seen people show others how steps of a process can be altered and even eliminated to improve productivity. Many ideas have generated better quality products, as people who work with the product directly notice improvements to ensure that only the right items leave the building.

I have stopped being surprised that most employees on a team will actively speak to wanting only the best products to leave the building. It has taught me and other managers around me that it would behoove us all to realize how much pride people do take in their work. If someone spends his or her day making something, that person certainly doesn't want to knowingly disappoint a consumer (much less our customer). Yet many managers have expressed surprise at this. Ideas can be methodically gathered as they relate to the specific aspects of the overall process.

Capability Number 4: Seeing the Big Picture

Workers generally have limited roles in their job functions, which consequently limits their vision of the whole organization that they support. Lean principles use Process Management as the foundation of understanding how each step links to the next, to meet the customer's needs in the end result. The understanding of the steps helps identify wasted parts of the process, which improves results as well as better meets customer needs.

For example, I was working with a group of employees on understanding the customers they work for in their daily production work. We exposed the employees to the sales and marketing issues, the product development challenges in choosing the right ingredients that make products that sell well, the purchasing challenges to make sure we have the right amount of the right ingredients for the customer, and then the distribution concerns related to getting the product to the customer on time and in good condition. As the employees became more aware of the parts of the process that precede production and come afterward, they became more sensitive to how their frustrations link to problems bigger than their own departments. They became more willing to participate in problem-solving efforts and being more open to new ways of doing things.

The customer also found this team approach covering their whole process impressive in terms of feeling like our people truly understood the total challenges. When the customer would visit the plant, the team members would present their problems and solutions as a whole group covering sales, marketing, product development, quality, distribution, and production. The customer found a great deal of work had gone into making the product better and more effectively, so issues they could help with were easier to address. Therefore, accessing people's ability to change is critical to achieving the vision as a whole.

Capability Number 5: Solving Problems

People possess considerable wisdom, judgment, and creativity that can help any organization solve a wide range of issues or problems. Continuous improvement and Lean cultures are built on team-based problem solving that attempts to tap into these human abilities.

For example, when I originally learned to structure problem-solving teams, it was important to understand how to teach people to effectively lead these teams as well as what it meant to be a member of these teams. Problem solving involves analyzing a situation, often using intuitive abilities as well as logical thinking. Solving problems also involves both analyzing data and creating a range of solutions to evaluate the best options.

However, many jobs do not often involve any responsibility to solve problems, especially in nonmanagerial roles. The common view is that the majority of workers *create* problems that the chosen few (i.e., their managers) must then solve.

Coordinating problem solving in a daily work flow also requires new types of processes to handle the extensive abilities of people to identity and resolve issues. HR could be a significant support with facilitating daily problem solving; unfortunately, HR is typically not involved in such activities.

Capability Number 6: Working to Meet Visible Common Goals

The failure to have people strive to meet goals using visual measurements is a waste of their ability to seek accomplishment. I was walking through one of our facilities the other day, and I asked a manager if his people knew what he was concerned with each day. The manager replied, no, his people had no information about the goals he was trying to achieve. The manager also agreed that if the people knew the levels of scrap he was trying to achieve, the productivity levels he was being held accountable for during the week, and the quality concerns raised by the customer that they would likely be of much more help to him in getting these goals accomplished. It just hadn't *occurred* to him that involving the 40 people in his department in the goals would help him at all!

As he then put the goals on the board each day, he not only noticed that his goals were achieved but that the employees were easily engaged in his concerns as they became aware of them. The people were also quite pleased when they hit his productivity goal, and they all celebrated the following Monday with a special lunch.

Continuous improvement cultures almost always *measure progress for all to see.* People are not only capable of understanding current levels of performance, but instinctively seek to surpass those levels to meet goals.

However, managers typically do not see a reason to ensure that everyone knows the goals and the progress towards meeting them. But how well can a person do a task without any feedback on his or her progress? People need a gauge to let them know if they need to adjust to do better. HR could play a significant role in designing and educating people on the visible measurements that will help them see their results as well as what to adjust in order to make even more progress.

Capability Number 7: Demonstrating Personal Leadership

Failing to allow people to take ownership of their work is a waste of their ability to demonstrate personal leadership. In contrast, continuous improvement cultures *require* people to be engaged with their results.

When I was first introduced to this concept, it related to changing quality checks to the "point of manufacture" instead of it being done afterward. People who made the product were required to ensure the product met specifications and that they knew how to check it themselves. This change in personal leadership produces better results with customers, championing changes and being a role model for others. People accomplish what they feel *ownership* towards. Yet managers who are concerned for their positions will not seek to create more leaders. Consider the role HR could have in inspiring employees to take ownership or show their leadership.

Conclusion: Wasted Talent Is a Natural Result of Failed Culture Changes

Not only do Lean principles illuminate the way to uncover capabilities in your workforce, they are also the best foundation for successful culture changes. Figure 1.1 reflects how these seven Lean principles will be reflected in many of the upcoming chapters of this book. This repeated threading of the Principles provides a model for how improvement efforts or Lean implementations could successfully implement ways for people to contribute more in their daily work.

Chapter 2 will outline why culture change efforts fail and how these failures are again founded in a lack of real consideration for the dynamics of getting more from your people. The opportunity to better understand culture change and how to create a workplace where people contribute most of their capabilities would not marginally enhance results; it would change the possibilities for an organization entirely. In other words, it would change the game. Both of these concepts are the foundation for what Lean HR is devoted to solving as it strengthens the participation of HR in addressing these issues.

Integration of Seven Common Lean Principles

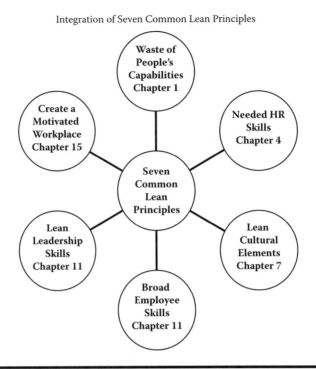

Figure 1.1   Integration of seven common Lean principles.

CHAPTER 1 SUMMARY

KEY IDEAS

■ The greatest waste within an organization is underutilizing the abilities of people.

■ The underutilization of people's talents and abilities is due to prevailing attitudes, limited work roles, and the need to create new methods to channel people's full potential.

■ Using seven Lean principles as a framework, the missed opportunity with people includes the failure to have them:

1. Work with the customer in mind.
2. Learn from mistakes.
3. Identify concerns.
4. Improve results
5. Solve problems
6. Measure progress.
7. Provide personal leadership.

Wasting people's abilities results in dissatisfied customers, repeated mistakes, unidentified problems, and unengaged team members who wait for someone else to fix everything. These issues can lead to the loss of jobs, businesses that fail by not meeting financial or other significant commitments, not to mention the loss of human potential.

STRATEGIC QUESTIONS FOR HR

1. What problems in *your* organization could be the result of some or all of the wastes of your people's abilities?

   _____

   _____

   _____

2. What attitudes would need to change to better utilize the people in your organization? What new processes would need to be created? How would work roles need to change?

   _____

   _____

   _____

3. What gains would your organization experience if you could improve the use of your people's abilities?

   _____

   _____

   _____

LEAN HR IMPLEMENTATION ACTIONS

1. Using the ideas generated above, evaluate the current level of utilizing the talents of the people in your organization. Create action plans to begin processes to optimize human potential.

   _____

   _____

   _____

   _____

   _____

   _____

I generally create these plans with teams by asking team members to identify potentially new requirements for jobs that go beyond the basic tasks of the work. Following is a list of items that might generate specific areas to change:

1. Requiring people to demonstrate proficiency in problem solving.
2. Participating in problem-solving teams.
3. Participating in their natural work group as effective team members.
4. Demonstrating proficiency in the overall process.
5. Identifying what skills could be added to jobs.

The action plans would be first based on strategic changes to job content. Once the job changes are identified, then the action plans need to implement the change in a methodical manner. Once implemented, the affected employees need to be given the training and resources to develop the skills they need. Managers need to hold people accountable for the new skills and job requirements. The management team also needs to consider what other issues will arise from enlarging the jobs. More about this topic will be covered in Chapter 11.

2. Consider the benefits to your customers, employees, and the business as a whole from these changes. Draft the expected return from these changes to your organization. Consider your current quality requirements with your customers. How might having people contribute more fully affect your quality levels? How would you measure the improvement?

_____

_____

_____

_____

_____

Chapter 2

Attempts to Create an Improvement Culture Often Fail

The waste of people's abilities has been the main focus of Lean, or continuous improvement, efforts. Yet many (if not the majority of) improvement initiatives have failed to achieve expected results over time because the efforts never achieved substantial changes in daily behaviors. This chapter begins with the excuses companies make about why they say their efforts fail and then explores the real reasons. Lean efforts have failed in the past due to a lack of approaching the process as a complete cultural change. The reasons for failure can be offset with success factors that have strong links to areas of HR, making it an important aspect of why HR must be involved.

Common Excuses for Failed Lean Efforts

When frustrated with results, some people believe that the problem is with their particular organization:

- "We aren't structured to do Lean."
- "We don't have the right people to do Lean."
- "We can't use continuous improvement methods because our products and services aren't appropriate for these applications."
- "Lean doesn't work for us."

However, close examination of continuous improvement practices reveals that a company's size, industry, organization, and production type are likely *not* linked to the reasons for the failures of these initiatives. As some organizations have pursued and been frustrated with the results from Lean or continuous improvement initiatives, they ultimately realized that they may not have fully invested what was needed to effect change over time. In questioning the level of investment, many organizations point to a simple answer for their failed results. Here are some examples of these simple answers:

■ "Senior management was not involved."
■ "The training was not sufficient to teach the methods."
■ "The whole group was not involved in the training."
■ "The team in charge of the Continuous Improvement Program was poorly led."

But these simple answers don't address the root problems. In contrast, organizations that are successful with continuous improvement look much beyond these simple excuses and seek broad applications of these theories—more commonly known as the *culture* of an organization. If Lean or continuous improvement projects have failed to deliver, many organizations have reached the conclusion that cultural changes are required for sustainable results. A Lean organization that improves over time requires focusing on changes in daily behaviors, as opposed to specific Lean projects. Lean HR provides a thorough examination of a wide range of programs and processes that, when added together, create the level of investment required for long-term success.

Reasons for Failed Lean Efforts

I have met managers from many organizations that claim their failed improvement efforts are due to the fact they have over relied on *"Lean methods"* as well as have issues with *sufficient leadership support* to create the changes in daily behavior that would create longer term improvements in their results. The first issue is based on the idea that continuous improvement theories or Lean tools *are not capable of* providing significant results over time or these theories do not apply to particular companies or industries. Instead, previous efforts have failed due to a failure to understand the required investment in time, leadership, and resources to achieve successful results.

Reason Number 1: Applying Lean as a Set of Tools

Some companies reason that continuous improvement or Lean methods are merely fads and that these theories do not deliver sustainable results. During many visits with organizations that follow Lean methods for their overall business improvement efforts, I have often heard that the operationally oriented projects have been successful, but have still not equated to the desired results.

For example, I recall an organization commenting during a tour of its facility to learn about continuous improvement that although the Lean projects were successful at the time, a year later, the efforts often cannot be seen in the daily activities. Another organization stated that its training efforts were not successful within a short time because that organization did not seem truly ready for the behavior changes proposed in the training materials.

In talking with dozens of organizations working on Lean implementations, numerous discussions described their overall dissatisfaction with long-term results, with the best answer to date being that a cultural change is required for long-term benefits. The conversations have highlighted that change efforts have simply not been adequate for sustainable results.

In addition, the significance of the improvement results, in terms of material impact, has often been questioned. I've seen many organizations cease their continuous improvement activities because they were disappointed in the results. This has led some organizations to conclude that the tools are not adequate, raising the question as to what is beyond the tools. Beyond Lean tools refers to a range of activities that support a Lean culture. The primary difference is that the tools are applied during a training exercise or on a project-by-project basis. Lean is effective as a daily activity or a frame of mind that has no clear stop and end points. It's a way of working—not a specific use of a Lean approach (or tool).

Many programs fail because people go back to their regular work and don't use the same principles they had just learned in the "Lean program." For example, people might have been taught "Lean" problem-solving techniques on specific improvement projects, but then they fail to use these practices in their other work.

When I first learned continuous improvement principles, I had spent a whole week learning about where we had waste in our organization and how to root it out. Yet, within a year, many of the principles were not in use in a broad context but had been limited to the specific areas designated for "improvement" using the tools of the consultant. Over time, people blamed the consultant and the tools for being inadequate, and some wondered if we should have ever spent the money investing in this project. Yet it was obvious to me that companies I was visiting that used some of these same techniques, but used them every day in every situation to which they could be applied, found themselves *amazed* at the results. By looking at other companies, it showed me that the problem was likely in our limited application and not in the tools/theories themselves.

Companies are realizing that effective problem solving needs to be utilized in a day-to-day approach. Building improvement theories and tools into daily work is a significant part of building a continuous improvement culture. When benchmarking companies with very successful Lean efforts, I have found the devotion to the principles to be at a 10-year mark or better, with significant resources committed to supporting the cultural elements. In general, the approach to problem solving using facts and done in a team approach as appropriate is less of a *project* and more of a *daily approach* to accomplishing tasks. The more Lean cannot be separated from the organization as an effort or project, the more successful the results. The people working in those organizations wouldn't describe their results as from "Lean" because the work is fully integrated. They could point to improved customer satisfaction, better quality, better efficiencies, and hugely improved engagement by the majority of people in the organization—the largest success being the engagement.

Reason Number 2: Changes Require New Ways to Work

Lean efforts require changes in daily behavior that would certainly require HR to support and execute. New ways to work might include processes for gathering and implementing significant numbers of employee suggestions or empowering the workforce to make decisions and solve problems in new ways.

I have seen more than one organization truly struggle to get a handle on how to develop an environment of participation and channel the influx of ideas and suggestions without creating bottlenecks at the implementation of ideas. The ideas become quickly backlogged because there are not enough people sufficiently trained to implement the changes at all levels of the organization. Managers can quickly become frustrated at teaching a broader group of employees what it takes to implement ideas and how queries to expend cash are treated. In the long run, these efforts bear fruit by having more and more people aware of how the business is operating. In the near term, these new ways to work require management teams to create the new processes and work through a number of difficulties.

Patterns of behavior, by their nature, don't change easily. Individuals may require a significant amount of intervention to create new behaviors. In addition, conflicting messages work against the behavior changes by reinforcing old or undesired behaviors, which is in part why the absence of HR can be damaging. One significant change in the new ways to work includes a change in the balance of power from changes in leadership roles.

Reason Number 3: The Balance of Power Creates Resistance

The balance of power creates resistance to changing behaviors for productivity improvements. Because the benefit is obvious of involving more people in identifying and resolving problems, it's equally obvious that the mindset that resists this is well entrenched. Management's need to keep authority to a few is based on fears that those few would be replaced, or found to be unnecessary, if authority were released to the majority. Not only do paradigms exist as to why the masses can't be trusted to exercise judgment, but other paradigms also say chaos would reign if more people were involved. I've had managers tell me that they fear they would not have jobs if they teach more people how to do the reports they create, make the decisions they make, or solve the problems they currently handle. The challenge for me has been to show these same managers that they would have a *different* role to coach and teach people to do the tasks that are currently the managers' and that they would provide value in being able to have many people do their work instead of just themselves. These same managers require significant support in learning the new skills it takes to coach and teach—rather than perform tasks normally considered "management" roles.

Managers have often described their concerns about their employees' attitudes and how their employees would not be prepared to handle responsibilities currently handled by others. The challenge has been to show such managers how these same people make decisions elsewhere in their lives, and we need to continue to explore how more people can make better decisions while doing the work now.

I've also seen managers point to the person in their group who is most vocal and negative in his or her approach as if it represents the entire team. Yet, those managers are falling into a common trap of letting one person's opinion speak for others. Each team member is certainly capable of more than he or she is contributing, and our challenge is to find out just what their capabilities would allow for the benefit of the organization as a whole. These attitudes should not be underestimated in their effect on workplaces and ensuring that talent is severely restricted.

Reason Number 4: Lack of HR Involvement Automatically Risks Failure

Culture requires alignment to sustain momentum. When the entire HR program is in any way out of sync with the continuous improvement strategy, it damages the culture-related objectives being supported.

For example, I was meeting with an organization that was going through a large-scale change with how supervisors worked with employees, to generate new solutions to problems and to have everyone work together to improve their quality and efficiencies. The same organization left HR completely out of the training process and overall strategy. When supervisors were then failing to meet newly designated expectations, HR was not able to provide any type of support to understanding current job content, charting needed changes, supporting performance management or reward systems for current desired leadership behaviors. After all, HR programs drive messages from the time someone is interviewed and brought into the organization all the way through that person leaving the organization. Training, performance management, and rewards all provide information about what is important. When an organization's senior leaders clarify that HR has no significant role in creating the organization's culture of improvement, they are likely underestimating the damage that conflicting messages can do to the promotion of desired behaviors.

Now let's look at how HR has a key role in addressing the first three reasons, which in the end eliminates the fourth.

HR Has a Key Role in Successful Lean Implementations

Creating successful continuous improvement requires the resolution of many of the common reasons (or root causes) described so far in this chapter, which all make the role of HR clearer in terms of how it supports the success factors. Although HR is not likely the driving force behind Lean implementations, they cannot be fully successful without considerable involvement by HR with the work.

HR's Involvement with Cultural Implementations

Cultural implementations will involve building Lean principles into daily behaviors and attitudes. Because this work involves many aspects of day-to-day work, HR has an obvious role in building these ideas into the range of communications, activities, job content, and HR programs.

For example, if continuous improvement is built into daily meetings with employees, HR may support the training needed to conduct effective daily meetings in terms of communication and tracking employee suggestions. If problem solving with interdepartmental teams is part of a normal work day, HR may help facilitate these efforts and build them into the structure of regular meetings.

HR's Role in Designing Newly Required Processes

HR should be involved in implementing processes for handling new approaches to work. Many of the Lean principles require processes for handling employee suggestions and the changing roles of leadership. HR needs to be closely partnered with other leaders in the organization to design and implement processes that support employee engagement, problem solving, visual management, and team work. Many of the later chapters of this book describe in detail how HR can support the design and implementation of the processes needed to better optimize people's abilities and the corresponding momentum for enhanced results.

HR Supports Handling Resistance to Leadership Changes

Lean implementations involve significant changes to how leadership functions in an organization. As mentioned, there is significant resistance to these changes, because they are in conflict with what many leaders believe drives their employment security as being the one at the top with the answers and the knowhow to "run things." The changes also conflict with managers' common ideas about the limited abilities of the broader groups of people. Change management processes that deal with resistance must be utilized to address the significant resistance that emerges from the supervisory ranks, as they question their new role in a more efficient environment that more fully utilizes people. It's not that they have less of a role, but that they need to change how they work.

I have seen HR become very involved in restructuring a manager's job content, coordinate the evaluation of the current staff's skills, develop training plans for managers to develop needed skills, and help create a leadership vision that supports the majority of individuals in achieving goals, solving problems, and making better decisions. I have also used change management theory to analyze the resistance *one manager at a time* and address each individual's concerns to move the overall system forward. People cannot be *herded* into compliance with these changes.

New Roles for HR Apply to Any Organization

The goal of this chapter was to help you understand how Lean human resources can optimize an organization's—*your* organization's—continuous improvement initiatives. Yet, the nature of continuous improvement is simply the advancement of business results. However, even if an organization is completely unfamiliar with Lean or continuous improvement, these ideas equally pertain to them. Assuming most organizations are pursuing improvement of some type, these principles work towards the achievement of any mission and vision. Chapter 4 looks at how a new vision for HR can begin to create a foundation for providing the expertise needed to actualize more people in the workplace.

The Key to Unlocking HR Support of Successful Culture Changes

After considering how HR has a role with each of the key reasons for failed culture changes, we look forward to Chapter 3 for a description of how traditional HR departments lack the skills and vision to assist with culture changes and to make the strategic changes necessary in HR related programs that would make improvement efforts successful. Section II will also describe how a new vision for HR can begin to create a foundation for providing the expertise needed to actualize people in the workplace and create necessary changes for successful improvement cultures (Chapter 4).

CHAPTER 2 SUMMARY

KEY IDEAS

- Lean or continuous improvement initiatives have failed at a disturbing rate in achieving desired results over time.
- Although the cause of Lean or continuous improvement failure may be disputed, it is increasingly common to seek a culture of continuous improvement as the answer.
- HR is often not included in continuous improvement efforts as having significant leadership roles and strategy.
- Lean HR strategies can greatly improve results through driving sustainable cultural change.

STRATEGIC QUESTIONS FOR HR

1. Could the current role of your HR department and HR professionals be expanded to dramatically improve continuous improvement efforts in your organization? _____

   _____

   _____

   _____

   _____

   _____

2. What are reasons your continuous improvement efforts either have failed or might fail in your organization? _____

   _____

   _____

   _____

   _____

   _____

3. Does your organization approach continuous improvement on a cultural basis? _____

   _____

   _____

   _____

   _____

   _____

LEAN HR IMPLEMENTATION ACTIONS

1. Evaluate the success or failure of the continuous improvement efforts, including feedback from involved parties:
   - Describe your experience with any failed Lean efforts. _____
   _____
   _____
   _____
   _____
   _____

   - List the factors blamed for the failures._____
   _____
   _____
   _____
   _____
   _____

   - Do any of the factors match the real reasons described in this chapter? _____
   _____
   _____
   _____
   _____
   _____
   _____
   _____

2. Evaluate the cultural component of continuous improvement strategies:
   - List aspects of your continuous improvement or Lean principles that are practiced daily. _____
   _____
   _____
   _____
   _____
   _____
   _____

■ Describe how your Lean efforts are promoted in daily activities. _____

_____

_____

_____

_____

_____

■ List the processes that support your continuous improvement strategy. _____

_____

_____

_____

_____

_____

_____

_____

3. Evaluate the role of your HR department in the continuous improvement efforts that your organization has implemented:
   ■ What has been your HR group's role in the continuous improvement efforts? _____

_____

_____

_____

_____

_____

_____

   ■ What role could HR have in daily changes in behaviors? _____

_____

_____

_____

_____

_____

_____

_____

■ How have you involved HR in leadership changes? _____
_____
_____
_____
_____
_____

4. Evaluate how your organization's HR programs reflect the overall
continuous improvement strategies:
   ■ Describe how the leader-selection process supports the
   required leadership for Lean. _____
   _____
   _____
   _____
   _____
   _____
   _____
   _____

   ■ Describe what training HR has or has not provided to support
   the newly required skills. _____
   _____
   _____
   _____
   _____
   _____

   ■ Describe how the performance management system has been
   changed to reflect Lean principles. _____
   _____
   _____
   _____
   _____
   _____
   _____

■ Describe how the rewards or compensation systems have been changed by HR to reflect new requirements. _____

_____

_____

_____

_____

_____

_____

INVOLVING HR AS A BUSINESS PARTNER

If the waste of people's abilities is founded in attitudes and a weak HR department, then strengthening HR starts to address one of the main reasons for the underutilization of people. Therefore, the next four chapters focus on how to strengthen the HR department.

Chapter 3 reviews why the historical role of HR must be overcome for HR to create the type of contributions that will help organizations fully utilize the talent of their people as well as support a fully integrated culture that creates sustainable improvements. Chapter 4 begins by providing a new vision for the HR department to fully realize the abilities of each employee. Chapter 5 provides a glimpse of how to use traditional Lean methods as tools to improve HR processes, while strengthening the skills of HR managers at the same time. Last, Chapter 6 takes a look at how the HR strategy needs to be rooted in the organization's business strategy, and the HR implications for how Lean business strategies differ from traditional business strategies.

These four chapters roadmap a stronger HR department that will help illuminate the waste of people's abilities as they are able to bring forth the skills and plans to show what better utilization of people would provide. Table 1 shows the broad range of skills that need to be developed to begin to support Lean principles in the workplace (skills that will be covered in Chapter 4). Table 1 also reflects how Lean business strategies utilize the optimization of people in setting their future courses of action (which are covered in Chapter 6).

Table 1   Strengthen HR through Skills and Link to Strategy

Lean Principles	New Vision of HR Skills (Chapter 4)	Lean Business Strategy (Chapter 6)
Customer focus	Customer service skills Know sales process	Primary focus on customer
Continuous Improvement	Teach and facilitate Lean methods	Significant advancement in key results
Broad participation	Meeting formats, suggestion boards, etc.	Designed and executed with involvement
Process management	Facilitate and teach process mapping	Based on process orientation
Team-based factual problem solving	Facilitate and teach team skills and problem solving	Requires disciplined problem solving
Visual measurement of results	Teach and recognize visual goals	Goals and results are well communicated
Inspirational leadership	Wide range of leadership support	Requires broad-based leadership

Chapter 3

Keeping HR in the Background Is a Business Problem

Chapter 1 dealt with how companies are generally unaware of how they are wasting talent and have great opportunities to advance their organizations through better utilizing their people. Yet the failure to fully utilize the *department* devoted to people is directly related to the failure to utilize people *in the workplace.* Do you see your HR department as a team of professionals, a group to be relied on to achieve strategic goals? Does your HR department actively help improve employee productivity? Does your HR Department directly impact financial results?

The most common answers I get to these questions is "absolutely not." Yet most do agree that they would like to receive more value from HR professionals. Do you see the value HR could bring if they could provide expertise in developing people or directing behaviors towards strategic directions? This chapter looks at three key problems that keep HR in the background:

1. How the historical roles of HR get in the way.
2. How attitudes about people in the workplace hide the value of HR.
3. How many HR professionals lack the business skills to have more impact.

In looking back at business in general over the last 50 years, what are the roles you link with the Human Resources Department? I often have people refer to administrative-type tasks, such as ensuring that benefits paperwork is in order, making sure when people are hired that all the paperwork is done, or as a place for people to ask questions about their paycheck or benefits. Others link HR to overseeing union activities. Some of the most unpopular roles for HR professionals are as policing functions.

The link to the questions above is that if HR functions are tied mostly to administration, policing, and unions, it's hard to see HR professionals as contributing to the business strategy or having any financial responsibility (directly or indirectly). The fact that HR tends to be in the background is due both to how businesses view the department and how HR professionals present themselves. Many organizations give HR limited support roles and fail to assign anything of worth to this underutilized department. On the other hand, HR staff members tend to lack business consulting and customer orientation skills that can generate financial impact and strategic insights. In general, HR staff members do not seek roles that lead strategies or improve productivity in organizations, yet so much of these improvement efforts require the expertise and support of people-related programs. This chapter describes these traditional HR roles to show how limiting the HR department's role in an organization can contribute to the problem of wasted employee productivity.

How Historical Roles for HR Create a Problem Today

The HR department (often referred to as the personnel department) in many organizations hasn't changed all that much over the years—unfortunately, at least not as much as you might expect. Although the function of the department is clearly changing, the roots of it live on: originally, the HR department was in charge of filing records and handling developing laws around labor, and those functions have hindered HR from developing into a source of experts about *people as strategic assets.*

As mentioned, HR historically has been an administrative operation, a policing function, and the expert on union relations. These roles all have value, but they have been a poor substitute for the potential value of a department that should be more focused on *people.* The reason it is important to look at the historical roles of HR is that they are holding this function back today. Table 3.1 sums up their attitudes towards HR as well as their attitudes about themselves, which both need to be addressed for

Table 3.1 Traditional Human Resources

Common views about people and HR	Common attitude of HR towards themselves
Assigned role of HR	**Insufficient focus on HR skills:**
• Administration	• Business skills
• Policing policies	• Focus on financial reporting
• Union Relations	• Consulting skills
• Recruitment	• Customer orientation
• Basic Training	• Strategic skills
• Payroll	• Improvement skills
View of people in the workplace:	**HR concerns:**
• People are not an advantage	• "They won't let us do more."
• People have narrow job roles	• "They don't respect us."
Roles not assigned to HR:	**HR often does not seek:**
• Strategic driver of capabilities	• Strategic roles
• Driver of productivity	• Productivity related work
• Key positions in improvement	• Leadership for improvement
How do these issues and attitudes impact each other?	

HR to achieve a strategic role. It's not just a matter of pulling HR out of the background. Why do the historical roles hold HR back?

Root Cause Number 1: Too Much Focus on Administration

The roots of the HR function originate in "personnel management" as an administrative operation. "Personnel" is associated with keeping track of everyone within the organization. Organizing a range of information about employees, including their benefits and payroll information, has been a cornerstone for what actually could be a potentially strategic function. How can HR become more of a business partner, instead of only an administrative function?

Unfortunately, HR as an administrative function has led to relatively low skill levels of some HR professionals, especially as this paperwork has been a core piece of work and often seen as unavoidable.

Root Cause Number 2: HR Is Seen as a Policing Function

Many HR departments have also traditionally been seen as a policing function. As a "policing department," HR is in charge of making sure people follow rules, policies, and procedures. While some of these duties do have considerable value, they also can detract from creating the consulting relationships that would support having much greater merit. HR as a policing function is in direct conflict with being a business partner, because it often has HR in the role of saying "what *can't* be done," instead of what *can* or *could* be done.

Root Cause Number 3: Not Much Strategic Value Covering Union Relations

HR has also handled union relations as this role gained importance over the last century. Union relations were originally based on enforcing rules that were created for organized labor. However, as the economy has struggled in the last decade, some portion of organized labor has also changed to accommodate current requirements. The link to problems with organized labor has only further kept HR from being linked to people as a *positive* force for business results, instead of focusing on problems to be managed. The concept of HR as being in charge of union relations has also fed the idea that the HR function is primarily a policing function.

Attitudes about People in the Workplace Are a Problem

A bigger issue than not appreciating the potential value of HR as a strategic partner is that many organizations often do not see the real value of people in general. As discussed in Chapter 1, *people are the greatest asset that an organization puts to waste.* Traditional HR supports the idea of being a department devoted to people, but with little practical application of expertise that utilizes this positive feature. The "people department" is devoted to keeping track of people, but it's not supportive in advancing the valuable benefit of individuals to an organization and, subsequently, to its customers. Is that true in *your* organization? Let's take a look at the facets of this problem.

Root Cause Number 1: People Are Not Viewed as a Strategic Advantage

Not only do many organizations lack a realistic view of people's abilities, but they also miss the potential of people as being a strategic asset. Think about how *your* organization would benefit from considering how people are in fact a strategic advantage. Are your people seen as completing narrowly defined roles? Are your people simply executing whatever strategy steps are agreed on, or can they push the line and become a strategic lever? Organizations often overlook the possibility of people being a strategic lever in their marketplace or don't fully appreciate what this may mean.

The Ritz Carlton is one hotel our organization has benchmarked in terms of its approach to customer service. It's not enough to have just a great-looking hotel. People want premium service—which means when you ask a question, an employee doesn't leave your side until you have your question answered or you are with the right person to answer it. Answering people with "I don't know" is not acceptable conduct for housekeepers or someone at the front desk. This is an organization that realizes the training and attention to inspire their entire staff to provide great service is what will make its brand strong.

Root Cause Number 2: HR Has an Assigned Role (Which Doesn't Include Strategy)

As described previously, many organizations still commonly assign only an administrative or policing function to HR. Even if the HR staff members do have strategic skills, there is often a negative bias towards using those skills.

For example, I have mentored HR managers who are frustrated that when they venture an opinion about how changing the approach to developing people or how jobs are structured could have strategic impact, they find that others seem to dismiss their views. I have advised these managers not to be overly dissuaded from having a role at the strategic table, and to use wisdom in ensuring they add value that can't be dismissed to strategic conversations.

Root Cause Number 3: HR Is Not Part of Improvement Strategies

If HR is not a strategic player in your organization, then the department is not a part of any improvement strategy or the development of methods for how that strategy be deployed. The impact of keeping HR away from improvement initiatives is what creates irrelevant HR programs, and at the same time greatly limits the attempt to optimize people. At best, this function views the benefit of these efforts as a way to *reduce problems,* with little focus on the potential the HR department could actually bring. Therefore, these organizations do not see HR as a catalyst for encouraging people's abilities. They do not see HR as a driver of improvement efforts, either. Does this sound familiar in *your* organization?

Insufficient HR Skill Levels Don't Help the Issue

Another problem is that some HR staff members lack the skills that provide significant value. Many HR people are often unskilled as managers within the workplace, specifically from a business perspective. Some HR professionals lack strong interpersonal communication skills that complete their roles. However, low skill levels are accepted based on a sense that there is little at stake, given the low value placed on the function as a whole. Let's take a look at some of these skills—and think about how *you* could improve these skills in *your* organization's HR department.

Root Cause Number 1: HR Professionals Are Not Required to Have Strong Business Skills

Companies that don't value people also do not require HR professionals to have financial skills, political savvy, or business knowledge. This shortsightedness will not allow the company to recognize the range of financial loss or missed opportunity resulting from low skill requirements from the HR department.

Each organization that I've helped with HR has only had the experience of HR not being a value-add to the business strategy. Yet if you look at the cost associated with this department, having HR merely administrate, reduce risks, and handle union relations can be short sighted and leave a broad range of people issues and opportunities left untapped. As I've transformed the HR function, it historically began as a personnel department, which handles hiring, benefits, policy issues, and processing the paperwork of terminations. Beginning with adding more value as a partner against any business strategy, I've had my teams support the implementation of strategies from a people perspective.

As soon as there have been opportunities to support business improvement efforts or Lean implementations, I've been able to have HR add much more value by changing how people work in terms of reducing waste and meeting customer needs. Yet these changes have required the HR managers in place to build more business skills or to be replaced by people who are more prepared to fully participate in the business processes they support.

Root Cause Number 2: HR Professionals Lack Consulting Skills

HR people often complain about the lack of value placed on the HR function; they may feel overpowered by others in the organization. HR is not often aligned with other functions. HR may develop its own programs, but the programs often do not match what other key departments seek to accomplish for their strategic goals. I've heard of cases where HR developed entire leadership training programs that failed because of competing business needs.

I've seen HR develop whole leadership training programs that they struggle to gain participation in because of competing business needs. Yet the business leaders often fail to see how this leadership training program would actually help them achieve any of their goals or objectives, so it's no wonder they don't make the training a priority. HR can often fail to ensure their programs have a direct impact on the objectives of the workforce or management teams—which is why they end up seen as side shows or "nice-to-have" options but not critical to any important initiatives. Alignment is underestimated in its overall value. This lack of alignment is often one crucial way that HR professionals stand back and view themselves as undervalued and overlooked.

Root Cause Number 3: Many HR Professionals Lack Customer Orientation

The traditional HR department does not see employees as its *customers*—yet that's exactly what they are! The historical role of administration, policing, and union relations generally means that "personnel" is a support function with a limited value—a type of necessary expense to doing business. Keeping track of employees or ensuring that rules are followed does not consider whether the employee gets any value from the Personnel Department. If there is little awareness of employees as internal customers, HR will fail to optimize services as seen in the role of HR as business partner.

For example, one of the first HR teams to which I taught the concept of internal customers was so surprised at the idea of employees as customers that they asked me to lunch to discuss this idea. During our lunch, they discussed how they had been taught that employees were coworkers, and they were often frustrated that these coworkers failed to carry their weight with administrative tasks and didn't follow their rules properly. As I painted a picture of "employees as customers" and that our role is to meet their needs, their eyes grew wide in disbelief at the difference between that view and how they saw people around them. I talked to them about how it's similar to our external customer relations: "the customer is always right." Our job is to find ways to work with employees that feel good to them and add value.

As the members of this team later transformed their role in the organization, they noticed all that frustration dissipate as they challenged themselves to meet the needs of their customers and found pride in themselves when people complimented their service. They realized the roles of policing and dictating policy were not very rewarding. In contrast, being champions of supporting employee needs, as well as key business needs, was a role well worth pursuing. I find it endlessly rewarding to watch HR people transform their views of employees to customers and to challenge themselves to increasing heights of customer service.

Root Cause Number 4: HR People Do Not Seek Strategic Roles

In addition to how HR is underestimated by other departments, many HR professionals themselves are not clear about their role, and why they would request a seat at the strategic table. Many HR professionals view themselves only in their *historical, traditional* roles, and they may not have had a model or vision for *how they could add strategic value*. As HR professionals come to the table representing what can't be done and also the implication of organized labor, their role is undermined by their own conduct.

The changes in HR need to be more strategic and require HR professionals to not only to redefine their role, but also to be prepared to behave differently in leadership roles. HR professionals have an obvious benefit to provide, because they are exposed to everyone within an organization. That puts them in a great position to gain insights into cultural concerns, and also to generate information about problems that need resolving. HR can work on processes throughout the organization in terms of job design, employee roles, and cultural initiatives. In a way, HR sets the stage for the organization, and might be considered best as being the stage director.

For example, I was recently working with an HR manager of a major food company, who mentioned how HR worked with the general managers of every division to devise people-related strategies to achieve their primary strategic goals. Their organization had sought to advance the role of HR to being a significant contributor to their success and realized they needed better people strategies to get there.

Based on all the preceding factors, it stands to reason that traditional HR is not linked to productivity or other improvement efforts. The common roles for HR are restricted to primarily handling policy issues and other basic HR functions, often with little thought to the strategic implications of these efforts. Even many organizations with fairly mature Lean programs would still be puzzled as to what HR could add to their efforts. I've been surprised to see how often HR managers fail to see the cost to their reputation and ability to add value by failing to seek leadership roles with productivity or other improvement efforts. So let's take a look at Chapter 4, which presents a new vision for HR and the role it can play in the success of improvement efforts.

CHAPTER 3 SUMMARY

KEY IDEAS

- Traditional HR is rooted in roles as a policing or administrative function and handling union relations.
- The historical roles lead to HR professionals lacking core business skills that would enable them to have more impact in the workplace.
- The underutilization of HR comes from both the organization's view of HR as well as HR professionals' view of themselves.

STRATEGIC QUESTIONS FOR HR

1. Does your HR function match more with the "traditional" role of HR as shown in Table 3.1?
2. Does your business fail to see the talents and abilities of its people? How might seeing people as a strategic advantage be an area of opportunity for your organization?
3. What are the strategic implications related to people in your business? How could HR add value to the strategy in matters pertaining to people?

LEAN HR IMPLEMENTATION ACTIONS

1. Reflecting on the role of "traditional" HR, analyze the level of historical roles within your current HR department:
   ■ List the top 10 activities handled by your HR managers.

   1. _____
   2. _____
   3. _____
   4. _____
   5. _____
   6. _____
   7. _____
   8. _____
   9. _____
   10. _____

   ■ Which of those activities are linked to administration, policy oversight, or union related employee relations? _____
   _____
   _____
   _____
   _____
   _____
   _____
   _____
   _____

- If the percentage is more than 80%, how does that get in the way of your HR department adding more strategic value? ____

_____

_____

_____

_____

_____

_____

_____

Note: As you continue to build on the concepts in later chapters, you will develop ideas on how to redesign work related to historical roles so that it does not dominate the HR function. By the end of this book, you will also be able to analyze what value HR people do or do not bring to the work environment.

2. Define the weaknesses in the HR department that come from roles related to administration, policy enforcement, and union relations:
   - List the top 5 characteristics managers in the work environment assign to HR.

   1. _____
   2. _____
   3. _____
   4. _____
   5. _____

   - For each characteristic, assess if they relate to having HR partner for better results. _____

_____

_____

_____

_____

_____

_____

■ What would be the 5 characteristics you would like to see linked to HR?

1. _____
2. _____
3. _____
4. _____
5. _____

■ Describe the cost to the role of HR of being closely linked to the historical roles of administration, policy deployment, and union relations. _____

_____
_____
_____
_____
_____
_____
_____
_____

Chapter 4

A New Vision for HR

A number of forces are merging together that are shaping the future of HR into a crucial element in the achievement of improvements in the workplace. As mentioned in Chapter 1, challenges continue to escalate, causing a growing interest in reducing waste. The reduction of waste and competition in the marketplace will continue to point toward the need to optimize people, which is significantly more difficult than just reducing labor. The need to reduce waste and strengthen relationships with customers to increase and protect revenue also creates a pressure to ensure that *all* support departments, including HR, have a direct impact on results instead of being a cost of doing business.

These factors are creating a new vision of HR as a business partner that is required to contribute to results—financial or otherwise. As described in Chapter 3, previous HR roles that have existed primarily under the heading of "Personnel" have not been known to have much direct impact on financial results or other key objectives.

The new vision is also based on a much different view of the value of people. As business changes attitudes towards people, it will change the expectations of the HR department and professionals in this field. These changes will create a need for business partnering that requires HR professionals to have vastly different business skills than they have had to previously possess, as shown in Chapter 3. As HR professionals acquire more skills, they will seek new roles as they gain strategic presence and are prepared to advance productivity and improvement efforts. This chapter describes the new attitudes that will shape HR and the corresponding skills and roles that HR professionals need to develop, including some guidelines on how to develop these skills and roles.

New Attitudes about People Impact HR

Recognize that People Really Are a Competitive Advantage

Businesses such as Southwest Airlines and 3M bring to mind the benefit of making their people a competitive advantage. I have always had more comfort flying with Southwest personnel all over the country because of their culture of humor that is common in many of their flight attendants. I initially chose this airline because it was more fun to fly and because of other aspects of their customer service. Similarly, 3M is another company that took innovation to a new level by encouraging its people to generate ideas.

Businesses need to build a better understanding of what it really means to utilize people as a competitive advantage. The idea that "people make all the difference" or that they are the "greatest asset" needs to evolve into more than just words. Many strategic objectives link to people's abilities: service levels, innovation, or the ability to deliver goods and services at a low cost.

For example, consider the many industries that have multiple competitors. One primary factor that can set companies apart is whether the work standards of the people or a people-centric culture is seen as a competitive advantage. I have experienced this in one company that depicts this approach as I've rented cars in various cities across the country. Over time, I've found that Enterprise has a markedly different attitude of service, which has brought me back to them time after time. For example, one day, I was late coming to the airport and had little time to wait to ride the shuttle to the gates. The Enterprise attendant actually took me over the airport himself. And I've been hooked ever since. The focus on service is obvious in this rental company and has certainly affected my loyalty to it.

The top performer often has people strategies that are superior, with equally superior performance. This developing attitude that people are a competitive advantage will call HR to partner with the business to create the people management systems that can support this type of strategy.

Broaden Your Definition of "Labor"

In the future, labor will need to be defined more by potential contribution, rather than direct expenditure associated with tasks as cost factors. Because people as assets are capable of doing more than the tasks assigned, the developing appreciation of their abilities will call for encompassing a broader value. While the mechanisms for broader views of the value of labor are evolving, the need to achieve more through people will continue to require management teams to think differently about the value of labor.

I originally came across this idea when just learning about continuous improvement. Our organization had positions defined such as "packer," "driver," and "operator." The job definitions were strictly a matter of assigned tasks, and there were no other additional requirements. One major change was redesigning the job content to include more of people's abilities: the new job descriptions included teamwork, problem solving, decision making, and quality checks. The other major change involved extensive cross training, which provided most positions with familiarity with more aspects of the overall process.

The results of these changes were more than productivity; they included better levels of quality from successful team problem solving and overall teamwork. We were also able to significantly reduce the work force and meet increased productivity demands. The quality of the product improved because the prior "packers" became experts at their own quality standards and were in communication with others in the process when they noticed issues.

The expansion of the value of labor will require HR to partner with business to create people management systems that expand job roles and build in more cross training to allow for better process management.

New Demands Drive More HR Skills

The new attitudes that will shape HR professionals also require the development of new skills, in order to be stronger business partners with other line managers in an organization. Let's take a look at each of these skills, in detail.

Develop Business Strategy Skills

As mentioned in Chapter 3, some HR professionals have backgrounds that are either administrative or rooted in policy applications, more so than other business managers. However, the HR function needs to attract and develop talent with broader business and abilities, so they may support key business goals and objectives. These skills involve having an understanding of the overall strategy being employed and what is involved in deploying the objectives.

Some of the larger companies with leading-edge practices have used HR in powerful ways to bring forth their approach to quality and management. For example, Jack Welch of GE was well known be to be a believer in the importance of a strong human resources department. Southwest Airlines is well known for its people practices. And Motorola and GE used HR to build their Six Sigma efforts.

At the end of this chapter, several methods will be presented for attaining these and other essential skills for business partnering.

Develop Finance Skills

Financial reporting, costing, and key metrics are all part of the financial skills that an HR professional needs to keep up with his or her counterparts for effective partnering. You can learn these skills from a range of resources, for example, via online education and through local colleges and universities.

One very successful director of human resources who worked for me had an MBA that she got at night while working full time. That education improved her computer skills, research abilities, problem-solving capabilities, and the ability to document her position on given topics. The MBA program also ensured her skills were built around several core business areas, including economics, marketing, operations, and computer applications. This same director was able to attain a position as vice president of HR based on these skills, which helped her effectively partner with business. HR professionals should be encouraged to build broad business backgrounds.

In addition, you might start out by simply meeting with your organization's internal financial managers to ensure that you and other HR professionals on your team understand the specific practices and concerns of your organization, including all related key measurements of all strategic objectives. HR needs to be proficient in working with all key metrics to help align employees to the attainment of goals, which also involves consulting skills.

Develop Consulting (Alignment) Skills

In order to realize their full potential, HR must move away from historical roles (as described in Chapter 3). Also, HR professionals need to align with other core functions that are highly integrated with all functional groups. Success cannot be achieved within the HR department itself.

Consulting requires a constant awareness of how historical roles may interfere with internal client relationships. Providing expertise in how to work with people in new ways may be in sharp contrast to prior duties related to ensuring rules or laws are followed. Therefore, you need to be aware of how working from prior roles can affect the effectiveness of internal client relationships.

For example, suppose you have an internal customer who wants to terminate an employee because the customer isn't satisfied with the employee's performance. I've often heard people complain that the voice of HR sounds like "you can't do this…" or "you can't do that… ." In contrast, a consultative approach would include choosing from a wide range of options to resolve current performance problems. Working with the manager, you might turn the discussion towards the job content and look for a solution by changing that employee's job role. Or, you might discuss how interventions with training and coaching could resolve the problem. You might consider how managing the person differently could allow that person to be successful.

In short, you need to take a level of ownership to provide real value in resolving performance problems and not just report the legal guidelines. Therefore, you should handle the issue by making suggestions, and be conscious of tending to the client relationship, while you ensure that all applicable legal issues are being addressed. A comparison can be made to how an accountant or attorney might offer advice, in that the client may not like the message, but nonetheless values the messenger.

These consultative relationships need to be built with each core function of the business, including sales, marketing, quality, finance, and operations. These relationships might involve championing the execution of business programs or providing other critical support. The primary efforts need to be focused on the core functions, which require that HR goals match the main goals of both sales and operations to a significant degree. The nature of the goal statements may be different, but the efforts are moving in the same direction. Consulting skills serve as a basis for partnering with other departments, but to partner successfully, you need to develop integrated relationships with all other departments and you need to fully understand each group's current objectives, biggest struggles or problems, and its plans to accomplish its goals and handle those obstacles. Building consultative relationships with each department involves a high level of ability to have effective relationships, as described next.

Develop Customer Relationship Skills

At the heart of HR's relationship skills is the need to develop an appropriate sense of customer service. Customer skills for HR professionals need to encompass both an internal and external context. As mentioned in Chapter 3, upgrading HR services requires that you view all the employees in your organization as *your customers*. In contrast, also as described in Chapter 3, traditional HR departments and professionals viewed employees as either their coworkers or people who they needed to police.

As such, a new performance bar for business partnering is that employees are willing to pay for services received from HR. I first heard this term when our organization looked at how the support functions (such as finance, human resources, and administration) could tend to be "dead weight" on the bottom line because they neither sold product nor made product. The idea also included creating a paradigm shift that the goal needed to be making HR consulting abilities achieve a level they would be paid for, if need be, by the functions that requested the service. This change in mindset helped me understand that I needed to add value in such a way that if a department were to be asked to pay for my services, they would gladly pick up the cost as important to their goals (not a requirement).

As with any role, HR also needs to develop political acuity in developing relationships with key individuals, whose positions are able to "contract" with HR to develop significant initiatives, including the president, COO, VP of sales and marketing, and VP of operations. Just as a business is clear about its key accounts, an HR professional needs to be clear on his or her "key accounts."

Becoming aware of employees as your customers is critical to your success in becoming a true business partner in your organization. Optimizing people requires motivating them in an environment that cherishes all people's value. Customer service skills, such as building rapport and handling and solving problems, further creates an organization that drives customer focus into all activities.

For example, early in my career, I took a class in customer service that taught the importance of meeting the needs of the customer and to never say "no" to a customer. It has been helpful to me to always think of each employee as a customer and try not to say "no" but instead to seek some type of solution to that person's needs. This focus on service has been shown to be a good framework for building the right kinds of relationships with people to work towards common goals.

I also think of the entire organization as one long chain that leads to our customers. My role is to understand the customer at the end and to recognize that anyone I'm working with inside the organization directly impacts the customer in some way. As HR works with key customers as leaders of the organization and the person who works in production, both impact our customers.

The work of HR can also add value to external customers as well. One great approach to seeing the link between HR and external customers can be through certain kinds of teamwork, as shown in the next section.

Develop Team-Based Improvement Skills

Team skills include team leadership, facilitation, and membership-related skills. Continuous improvement or Lean implementations involve the need to facilitate teams. HR professionals can be trained to support cross-functional team activities, as well as management team activities.

My first Lean implementation had HR managers conduct Kaizen (our team-based improvement) activities; we began by evaluating the facility layout and making important process changes. HR actually located our outside support people to teach us how to do Kaizen activities, organized the timing of the activities, and then was able to facilitate them directly after watching the external consultants do them a few times. The operations manager was the customer of the work and the champion of the effort. The facility manager was pleased to have the help achieving his goals of productivity improvement and having HR take the ball to locate resources and support the people processes needed to change.

I've seen many HR professionals with strong training skills well suited to facilitate improvement teams once they learn the principles from participation on other teams.

HR can be a primary contributor in providing the instruction that it takes to deliver the training for team skills, including the ability to facilitate or teach others to facilitate team activities:

- *Team leadership skills* include knowing how to create both temporary and longer-term teams along with forming, maintaining, and completing team activities.
- *Team membership skills* are based on effective participation in team environments.
- *Facilitation skills* involve being able to support team processes as a neutral support to team dialogues, problem solving, and other team processes.

All these skills are involved in continuous improvement cultures; however, HR people have often not been involved in team-building skills. Moreover, many HR people have not made it a point to acquire these skills.

The new vision for HR calls for you to seek out ways to learn and practice team-based improvement skills on a regular basis. HR professionals need to make sure they get involved in any improvement activities that exist within the organization. Aside from participating on teams as a team member, pay attention to the skill areas that HR needs to support in terms of team leadership, facilitation, and membership.

HR can locate training materials from a range of sources that can be used in a facility. Although HR needs to contract with a group to provide these services, if HR offers to provide help in this area, they will likely succeed in becoming an integral part of the improvement efforts. In many organizations, operations takes on the training and skill development not because they generally want this job, but because HR is hanging in the background and not aggressively seeking their role in the work and seeing how they can add value.

Ensure Ongoing Personal Growth and Development

Ongoing personal growth and development differs from customer relationship skills because they involve any type of interpersonal interactions, not necessarily linked to a customer point of view. One obvious concern with HR professionals is whether they have above-average interpersonal communication skills. The professionals responsible for expertise in people matters need to be required to be exceptional at these abilities. These attributes involve listening, confronting conflicts effectively, and dealing with performance issues in a positive and supportive manner, among others.

I have worked on and honed these skills from the beginning of my career, and the results are an extensive ability to communicate through difficult situations, which has made a significant difference in my work results. I recommend managers who are struggling with people skills to regularly attend different types of interpersonal skills training. I've had managers who had problems controlling their tempers need interventions. Based on my own interpersonal growth work (which may have had different topics), I've come to understand how people can change a habitual behavior successfully. I've had other managers who come across in ways that detract from their relationships with staff members. My own growth process has helped me provide feedback to internal customers in a manner that helps them learn and feel supported at the same time.

In general, I find that people good at coaching others' behaviors have to have some experience with personal reflection and developments. My own development has helped me source training locations, support people in making a change to move past their barriers in interpersonal relationship skills, and be aware of how my own emotions or reactions can affect my views of situations (so they can be kept in check). Examples of training topics that have supported these skills include:

- Experiential leadership classes
- Dealing with conflict
- Dialogue
- Team work
- Dealing with difficult people
- Having difficult conversations
- Coaching conversations
- Dealing with fear in meeting goals

HR professionals would be well served to regularly complete interpersonal skills training in building these skills to a proficient level.

Develop Skill in Using Lean Methodologies

A range of newly needed skills is related to Lean implementations and is often referred to as the "tools" portion of Lean or continuous improvement skills. A few key topics would be the identification of waste and other opportunities for improvement, including value stream mapping with takt time observations, the use of Kanban systems, and other core Lean principles. The "tools" portion of Lean skills would considerably advance any professional's ability to support business objectives for any function. HR professionals are often not included in this type of training in organizations, because it is not obvious as to how they would help reduce waste or improve processes. Yet HR needs to become the voice of job design and would be well suited to see how process changes impact jobs and other aspects of work. In addition, HR professionals with strong training abilities would be able to teach Lean principles to people at all levels of an organization.

HR Needs to Step into New Roles

In addition to the new skills that HR professionals need to develop in order to contribute more to the organization as a whole, you should become familiar with several new roles as well.

Become a Strategic Partner

HR professionals will achieve more successful results when they are able to have a strategic presence. Focus your energies on ways you can help your organization increase revenues and decrease costs. First and foremost, ensure that you clearly understand the current strategy for your business and the key objectives that have execution plans to achieve the strategy.

HR professionals may do well to build their strategic planning facilitation skills to support this work in some organizations, if there is a need for this. Facilitating the process may help a HR professional become more involved in the business.

Next, for each strategic objective, consider what value you could bring to the process in terms of recruitment, training, accountabilities, recognition, and rewards. Consider whether each strategy being executed would further advance by more support from the HR function. Businesses with strategies such as building market share, competing through innovation, or lowering costs all have components that would benefit from professionals with an expertise in how to affect people. How can your HR department contribute to selling more products or services, driving down costs, or having a direct impact on the talent pool that supports these areas?

Become a Champion for Improvement

The HR function is a natural champion for improvement activities, because much of the support needed to change an organization's culture resides in HR programs. Although these efforts are a partnership with other teams, they require active and significant involvement from HR to be implemented. As a business partner, HR has an opportunity to step into leadership roles and be a champion for continuous improvement.

This role calls for more than just participation. Obviously, in order to play a lead role, HR professionals need to be inspired to lead this area as it builds a culture that will create better results.

How to Develop the New Skills You Need

Seek Out Educational Institutions

Education for HR professionals can include general business classes that build their ability to support strategic initiatives and fully participate in cross-functional teams. In addition, a range of coursework is available to build skills in the fields of organizational development, organizational behavior, leadership, training and development, systems thinking, and many others areas. I do encourage people who want to excel at HR to seek advanced levels of education to build the expertise to create interventions in the workplace that have impact.

Often when I'm helping HR professionals develop their skills, they look first to formal education. Although that is often a component of developing stronger business skills and more advanced abilities in the field of managing people, it's only one aspect of strong HR development.

Benchmark Yourself: Learn from Other Organizations

Benchmarking is a cornerstone of Lean or continuous improvement cultures. This practice involves locating organizations that have the best practices which are worth learning. The grass-roots approach of companies helping other companies provides a great opportunity for HR to advance the programs of their organization. For example, I am a member of the Association of Manufacturing Excellence, which is an organization that provides a wide range of benchmarking opportunities to tour other organizations and learn from a variety of experts. By visiting companies that have implemented best practices in a range of HR programs, I have learned about many of the concepts mentioned in this book. I am also a member of local HR associations and business associations that allow me to network with other organizations that have some best in class practices. Again, while formal education provides one type of information, some of the applications of business strategies are well supplemented with actual examples. It also provides a way to build momentum by actually using the methods of other companies to bring program designs forward faster based on what works elsewhere.

Find a Mentor

Beginning with business strategy, this area of management is not easily obtained from educational institutions without a significant investment of time, such as MBA programs. Another route to strengthen this area is for HR professionals to seek information internally in their organization through interview formats, which help them to gain more understanding of the strategies being pursued, as well as possible alternatives or prior failures.

Arranging conversations that outline key strategies in the business will help garner underlying and related information that helps to create foundations for accompanying HR strategies.

Once you've conducted interviews with your organization's internal subject matter experts, you can use other methods to learn about what they have learned. For example, you could research industry and related professional associations, seek additional internal mentoring, and look for other educational or training opportunities to develop a working knowledge of business strategies.

Join Professional Associations

A range of professional associations may help provide avenues for development and skill building in areas such as strategy, general HR, training, organizational development, and others. To build business skills, it might be advisable to join any industry-related associations to keep abreast of industry trends. Belonging to associations not only provides opportunities to attend functions that are educational, but also to mingle with other professionals, which provides additional opportunities for benchmarking and mentoring.

Assessing HR Skills

Figure 4.1 provides a format for evaluating the skills and experience of HR professionals. The rating can be done as a self-rating, by a manager, or by key customers. The rating would be more informative if it is accompanied by a feedback discussion to include specific examples, and a sense of which skill areas merit more of a priority at a given point in time or by a certain key individual.

Rate the following skills on a scale of 1 to 10. A rating of 10 means that the skill is fully developed and there is no need for additional development; a rating of 1 means there is no development in this skill.

Rating of 1–10:

1. Business strategy skills _____

2. HR strategy skills _____

3. Finance skills – financial reporting _____

4. Finance skills – key metrics _____

5. Finance skills – costing and controllable factors _____

6. Consulting skills _____

7. Effective relationships _____

8. Team skills – leadership _____

9. Team skills – facilitation _____

10. Lean skills – waste identification/removal _____

11. Advanced interpersonal skills _____

12. Professional associations _____

13. Benchmarking methods _____

14. Mentoring and feedback processes _____

Figure 4.1   Human resources professional evaluation.

CHAPTER 4 SUMMARY

KEY IDEAS

■ A new vision for HR departs from historical roles and places HR as a strategic business partner to other key functions.

■ HR as a business partner requires the function to add value and impact results directly.

■ HR professionals need to develop a range of skills, understand best practices, and develop effective relationships, in order to build continuous improvement cultures and partner with businesses.

■ Best practices are an integral part of building the HR function for the future.

STRATEGIC QUESTIONS FOR HR

1. Looking at Figure 4.1, does your HR function match more traditional HR models or the new vision for HR? _____

_____

_____

_____

_____

_____

_____

2. Could your business be improved with adding people as a strategic competitive edge to your strategy? _____

_____

_____

_____

_____

_____

_____

3. How are your current HR professionals suited to meet the skills, best practices, and relationship issues needed for both building a continuous improvement culture and partnering with the goals of the business overall? _____

_____

_____

_____

_____

_____

4. What is the impact of HR being less than qualified to meet the critical need of fully utilizing human assets across the organization? _____

_____

_____

_____

_____

_____

_____

LEAN HR IMPLEMENTATION ACTIONS

1. Consider how roles and activities from traditional HR impact current efforts. Lay out plans to handle traditional HR tasks differently. Administration:

   - What opportunities are there to reduce administrative tasks handled inside the organization? _____

   _____

   _____

   _____

   _____

   _____

   - Can any administrative tasks be moved to others with less strategic roles? _____

   _____

   _____

   _____

   _____

   _____

■ Can any administrative tasks be moved to direct supervisors to be more efficient and to allow them to build their relationships with employees? _____

_____

_____

_____

_____

_____

■ Can any of the administration be reduced or eliminated?

_____

_____

_____

_____

_____

Policy Management:
■ Do changes need to be made in how you or other HR professionals work with managers about policies to change their "policing role"? _____

_____

_____

_____

_____

_____

■ How can you involve more managers in policy developing and oversight so that it's not completely an HR role? _____

_____

_____

_____

_____

_____

Union Relations:
■ How are union relations impacting HR's strategic presence?

_____

_____

_____

_____

_____

_____

■ Is yours an organization that handles union relations that
   seem to damage your HR team's strategic presence? Are
   there other options that would either reduce the time
   involved or the role of HR that would strengthen their
   strategic position? _____

   _____

   _____

   _____

   _____

   _____

■ How can you make the approach to union relations more
   strategic in nature? _____

   _____

   _____

   _____

   _____

   _____

2. Reflecting on the new vision of HR, consider roles currently
   played by you or your HR professionals:
   ■ What opportunities are there to have a stronger strategic
      presence? *Describe the actions you would take.*
      – Facilitate strategic planning sessions? _____

         _____

         _____

         _____

         _____

         _____

      – Develop HR plans that support strategic plans? _____

         _____

_____

_____

_____

_____

- Meet with key strategic leaders and co-develop people-related plans that help meet strategic objectives? _____

_____

_____

_____

_____

_____

■ What opportunities are there to champion improvement initiatives?
  - Work with general management (CEO, president or chairman) on their vision for improvement? _____

_____

_____

_____

_____

_____

  - Work with operational leaders (COO or VP of operations, other senior level leaders) on their overall vision for improvement and how HR can help support this strategy?

_____

_____

_____

_____

_____

_____

  - How can HR have improvement initiatives within the HR department for its own for improvement, which also makes HR a champion for improvement? _____

_____

_____

_____

_____

_____

_____

_____

3. Create development plans against assessed skill level of current HR professionals based on the evaluation in Figure 4.1:

- Have HR professionals complete self-evaluations.
- Have senior-level HR professionals complete skill evaluations on staff members.
- Based on evaluations, develop three to five specific objectives to complete to improve the skills levels based on current priorities. _____

_____

_____

_____

_____

_____

_____

- Detail the objectives with specific actions and times for completion. *Include providing coaching and some type of support to HR professionals in creating and executing their plans.* _____

_____

_____

_____

_____

_____

_____

Chapter 5

Providing Better Service for Your Organization by First Improving HR Processes

Section I reviewed how having HR in the background is part of the reason companies commonly waste people's abilities, as one significant opportunity for companies to achieve greater results. Chapter 4 presented a new vision for HR, including the need for new skills and roles to meet the challenges involved with optimizing people. As part of the effort to strengthen HR, this chapter takes a look at how to improve each HR process as a foundation to succeeding at creating a new vision for HR. Finding the solution for how to develop a strong HR department certainly includes improving all HR processes. The purpose in redesigning and improving HR practices is threefold:

1. Ensure that each part of the HR processes adds value. When you remove waste and examine the value of each part of every HR process from an internal customer viewpoint, you create the time and resources for activities that have even greater impact on your organization's overall productivity and bottom line.
2. Remember—more engaged employees do better. When you ensure your customer base is satisfied to a meaningful degree, you create an environment in which the same customer/employees can do better work and hence drive better outcomes.
3. Learn principles of continuous improvement by practicing on HR processes. As you and other HR professionals practice Lean principles on

HR processes, you create a foundation so you can support the application of these principles in other departments elsewhere in your organization.

Each of these purposes is described briefly in the first part of this chapter, then the chapter provides an overview of how you can apply Lean methods to HR processes. The details of learning how to apply Lean principles to HR could be a book by itself. For the purposes of this book, this chapter provides an overview to give you a general idea of how to identify and remove waste, while improving the approach to meeting more customer/employee needs as you consider ways to improve HR processes.

Three Benefits of Improving HR Practices

1. Ensure That Each Part of an HR Process Adds Value

The purpose in having HR refine its own processes against customer needs is to ensure that each part of an HR process adds value. The process of adding more value to each part of the work frees up resources and removes unnecessary work, removing administrative waste as a primary objective, so you can redirect your resources to other work. Adding values for process steps are based on the following question, which will continue to arise during process improvement work:

If your organization's employees were paying customers, would they fund each part of every HR process? If not, why is this step necessary?

These questions help identify what work is really important, compared to steps that seem to have evolved into place, and that might be better if you either changed them or if employees simply didn't do them at all!

One of my early examples of this premise was uncovering that an entire clerical person's job was completely unnecessary because each item filed was located somewhere else and could be retrieved through an alternative method. This lesson taught me to question each task and look for alternatives before assuming the work needs to be done.

I've also seen examples where the work is needed, but it doesn't begin to add the value it could. For instance, I've seen HR people fill jobs using the fundamental steps of running an ad, interviewing candidates, and selecting someone to hire. Improving HR practices would then involve seizing opportunities that can be seen in measurable terms and by the improved perception of the overall organization, hiring managers, and candidates.

2. Remember: Happier Employees Perform Better

Another purpose of improving HR is to provide the best service possible to employees, making them happier and more satisfied. HR professionals can become frustrated that there is not more interest in their efforts. An underlying premise of some efforts is the premise "happier employees are more effective," which may not be widely agreed on by managers in the field. Even if the managers do agree, the development of happier employees may pale in comparison to activities with more visible and direct results. In fact, directly tracing employee satisfaction to measurable improvements can require a leap of faith.

However, there is much evidence that better overall financial results are found in companies that are considered above-average employers and that concern themselves to a great degree with the happiness of those employees. In addition, Lean principles are based on the dynamic of meeting people's needs within each process internally, which has customers more satisfied as a result.

3. Build Knowledge of Continuous Improvement through Practice

In general, I recommend first practicing Lean principles and continuous improvement methods in your own HR department, before you partner with other departments in their improvement efforts. Once you've learned to identify types of waste within your own HR department that will lead you to see it in processes in other departments. As you learn to improve HR processes so that internal customers are more satisfied, it becomes clear that valuable improvements are not simply cost-cutting measures. Working on improvement within the HR function needs to include time spent listening, observing, and considering factual data, which is more practice of skills needed for being a real champion of continuous improvement. As with all practices, it is better to ensure that the people in your group can do it themselves before you and they attempt to teach others in your organization.

Overview of the HR Improvement Effort

The steps to improve any set of processes begin with a broad overview of identifying opportunities. This analysis often includes the following activities:

- Reviewing financial reports
- Preparing reports on any related data
- Determining productivity measures

- Conducting interviews with people who work in the process or who are internal customers of the process
- Observing various activities
- Creating mapping processes (sometimes referred to as value stream mapping).

Similarly, process improvement for the HR function looks at areas that need improvement. Therefore, your analysis should include the following steps, listed here and described in detail in the rest of this chapter.

- Step 1: Evaluate HR for opportunities.
- Step 2: Prioritize your findings.
- Step 3: Execute your action plans.
- Step 4: Evaluate and revise actions once your plans have been in place for a period of time.

Beginning with Step 1 for evaluating opportunities, several activities may be involved in surfacing opportunities: let's take a look.

Step 1: Evaluate HR for Opportunities for Improvement

Clarify Current HR Processes

A process refers to a discrete number of steps or activities that, when linked together, create a significant result to an organization. Organizations function through a series of processes that work simultaneously to deliver products and services, including a wide variety of tasks within the support groups. In terms of the HR department, therefore, you should examine how *your* HR department handles the following functions or processes:

- Selecting, recruiting, and orienting employees
- Executing training and development programs
- Managing employee performance
- Handling recognition and rewards
- Administering benefits (which may comprise one or more processes)
- Managing payroll
- Conducting employee survey processes

Establish Process Boundaries

To first understand the processes you use in your department, make sure to note that every process has a *start point* and an *end point,* which clarifies what is included within the process as a whole. If you were working on improving the recruitment process, start by first agreeing on the start point and the end point.

■ The start point provides a sense of what creates the need that the process is designed to meet. Therefore, your recruitment process might begin at the point the need is identified by someone in your organization.

■ The end point provides information about the deliverable of the process. The end of the recruitment process would be when the need is fulfilled. One organization might stop the analysis of the process at the beginning of the selection process and another might stop once the selection process is completed. It only matters that you determine *up front* what piece of the process you plan to improve.

Because processes all link together, the cut-off positions may vary depending on the team conducting the analysis. However I have often been in process improvement teams that end up confused and frustrated about what parts of the process are being addressed. Teams have more success, and more importantly feel more successful, when they are clear about what is within the bounds of their team's efforts and what is not included.

Define Ownership, Results, and Stakeholders

Each process has a *process owner,* one or more *key results,* and *stakeholders* that are involved in the process. Let's look at each individually.

Identify the process owners. The process owner merits mention because an initial question of each process needs to be "who owns the process?" The owner is the person(s) with primary accountability who ensures the key result is achieved by the steps taken within the process. Often, many problem areas can be linked to confusion around who owns a particular process, so it's important to ask and answer this question about each process you examine.

In our example of working on the recruitment process, it may not be clear to people within an organization that this process is owned by Human Resources. I have seen confusion from managers who attempt to fill positions on their own without following prescribed processes. This lack of clear identification of recruitment as a process, with HR as the owner, helps support that confusion. On the other hand, I've seen that having HR more clearly own their processes with clear accountability helps prevent these types of poorly defined accountabilities around recruitment.

Determine the key results. The *key results* are another integral concept that links to *measurements.* In our example of recruitment, the key result would be a successful hire. In addition, each process needs to be measured. Yet, many organizations struggle to define "a successful hire." The measurements might include time to fill the position and the minimal length of time the person is employed with satisfactory or better performance ratings.

Although work often is conducted with little thought as to how it's measured, improvement efforts require the ability to measure progress. As such, the awareness of what measurement(s) merit attention is another early improvement step. At times, the measurements may not exist initially, and early improvement efforts actually involve developing the data and measurements to monitor the process going forward.

During the evaluation phase, examine the measurements of the current processes. This is not a time to create *new* measurements, but to canvas the environment for data that is readily *available*. Each process requires a measurement to assess the relative value or success rate of the process over time. As you evaluate a process for opportunities, you need measurements so you can establish the baseline for the current condition and to enable you to track improvements with the future condition.

Examples of these measurements in HR might include turnover rates, absenteeism rates, and satisfaction ratings. Turnover rates are generally the number of terminations over the opening level of people. Yet, questions may arise about which terminations to include. In addition, measuring the number of terminations doesn't speak to the cost involved. A more powerful turnover measurement might be to track the costs related to turnover to more clearly articulate the cost of this issue instead of a simple percentage rate.

I recently was working on this topic, and an HR team agreed that the cost of each termination was at least $2,000 for our most basic type of position. We realized that the cost of 400 terminations seemed to be worth reducing, given that the total estimated cost was close to $800,000. This cost was much more motivating than a turnover rate of 14%. Measurements should help make things more clear, not just provide a reference number.

Identify the stakeholders. Finally, *stakeholders* may be a broad category, and they may require consideration for effective improvement efforts. Stakeholders would include:

■ Corporate ownership interests (i.e., here, ownership pertains to the business itself, not of the process being worked on)
■ Customers
■ Various departments
■ External groups
■ Government agencies
■ Employee interests

Process improvement necessitates involving stakeholders in gathering information about the current process as well as any improvements made.

In our example of looking at the recruitment process, looking at the stakeholders helps illuminate what improvements will yield noticeable gains:

■ *Ownership interests* will want to have the best talent recruited into their organization and will want these people to be qualified for their positions.
■ *External customers* also care if recruitment is done well because they want to deal with the right people in the right jobs when working with the company.
■ *Internal customers* care that their needs are well met when they have recruitment needs.
■ *Departments* can end up with interests when recruitment needs go unmet or are filled inappropriately.
■ *Government agencies* are involved in ensuring recruitment is done without discrimination, in a fair and equitable manner.
■ *Employees* also stand to gain when recruitment is performed with more attention to needs and improvement.

Initially, the important step is to note the stakeholders of processes to ensure they are involved when appropriate. After establishing the processes, the next phase often involves gathering data and interviews with the customers regarding the broad range of HR processes to gain more understanding of the opportunities for improvement. In working on recruitment, an HR team might interview the ownership interest for insight into jobs that need more attention for strategic advantage. You might find that there is a particular role for which the talent in the job is particularly noticeable to the overall business.

For instance, I've seen instances where recruitment for particular kinds of engineering positions is critical. Improvement efforts found that increasing the attention paid to expanding the candidate pool for this role would benefit the overall business when engineering projects can be done better with better talent. Also, obtaining new business might be easier if the engineering talent pool is more highly regarded or has better backgrounds.

Talking to prior customers of the HR recruitment process is likely to uncover unmet needs that weren't discussed before because people accepted the service level provided. Upgrading HR services involves asking people what could have been done better to get better results, along with making the process easier on the people involved.

Gather Data about the Process You Want to Change

Gathering information is often done either in conjunction with the mapping process or apart from it. In general, improving an HR function requires gathering a wide range of information to assess how well the function is currently performing and to identify opportunities for improving it. Working on the recruitment process might include tracking data on all hires to assess time between requisition and hire dates, to measure the time to fill a position. Data on turnover rates might also illuminate the successfulness of the recruitment process.

Similar to other continuous improvement projects, process mapping is likely linked to gathering existing information, which may come from a wide range of reports that are developed both internally and externally by vendors. The recruitment process would have internal reports from the HR database on recent hires and terminations. Recruitment might not often include external vendors, but other HR processes often would involve outside suppliers.

For example, if you are working on benefits administration processes, external vendors might need to provide data reports on activity levels or other data downloads that can help better understand problems with the process. One way to organize the data is by HR process, to ensure each process is included in the reports, data, and measurements currently available.

Listen to Your Customer (Your Employees!)

HR needs to have customer input for superior program design work. The question of whether an activity provides sufficient value should not just be a general business question, but a question applied to each aspect of HR.

Employees as *internal customers* are one of the defining qualities of Lean HR or continuous improvement cultures.

Although employees are not *paying customers* in the traditional sense, they are clearly receiving benefits and services from your organization. Your employees can elect to purchase these services from a range of organizations (in other words, they can vote with their feet and find another job at another organization that does provide the benefits and services they're looking for!). Not only do employees vote by seeking work elsewhere, they more often become less engaged in their work when needs go unmet. As mentioned at the start of this chapter, HR has a key role in supporting a work environment where employees are highly engaged to create more successful results. Your employees have choices, just as external customers do. Therefore, when you're trying to identify opportunities in HR that could be improved, you should seek internal customer feedback, because that feedback provides the same benefits as assessing external customer feedback or satisfaction to improve services and satisfaction.

Gathering employee feedback may be done in interviews, focus groups, survey formats, or any combination of these. When you solicit feedback, you might ask employees to assess or rate current HR services, and you can ask for suggestions for new programs and enhancements to existing ones. Finally, you should gather feedback when you begin your process design work, and then gather additional feedback later to evaluate whether the changes or additions you're considering will be well received by the employees.

Create HR Process Maps

Generally, the evaluation phase begins with a prioritization of which HR processes are most in need of change. Redesigning even one process may require a significant amount of time. Therefore, when you're mapping an HR process, evaluate each step or activity within that process to ensure that each activity truly adds value.

Mapping involves diagramming each step of the process so it can be identified and evaluated. This is referred to as mapping the *current condition*. The map reflects a flow chart of a process; for example, the boxes shown in Figure 5.1 reflect key steps. Often, documents, systems, and people involved are noted for each step as laid out when gathering information. Improving HR programs then involves how you could redesign a process to add more value to the customer (internal or external). The map is eventually redone as a *future condition* as part of Step 2.

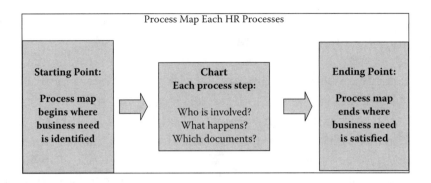

Figure 5.1 Basic process mapping.

Mapping is generally done in a team environment, for several reasons:

- To ensure that several perspectives are considered
- To ensure that people who touch the process at different points are connected in considering the current condition
- To ensure that the team works together and with external stakeholders to consider new ideas for the future

The team of people might include people outside the department for several reasons:

- To capture customer perspectives
- To include other support functions that are part of the processes
- To simply gain outside input

The purpose of mapping in a team helps gather perspectives along the whole process—which for many may be the first time they have ever shared their experiences at various steps in the process with each other.

Lastly, the acceptance of any proposed or implemented changes requires a wide range of communication to formulate ideas and approve them. The team has an enormous role to play in gathering feedback and communicating changes outside the team's work.

Step 2: Prioritize Your Findings

At the end of step 1, your team has a clear view of the current situation which will naturally have illuminated a number of changes that could be made to improve the process. Step 2 begins with the team generating an exhaustive list of possible changes that could be made to improve the results of the process being addressed. The end of Step 2 is having the team evaluate each improvement change as to whether it: (1) should be eliminated; (2) completed in the near term; or (3) is a good idea for the future. Other factors that are taken into account for the team to prioritize the list are described in the following sessions.

Identify Which Improvements Best Support the Business Strategy in General

Keeping in mind the key components of your organization's strategy, the team should evaluate how and where opportunities for improvement might impact the strategy most significantly.

Evaluate Improvements in Terms of Gains

Gains may be financial in nature or have other metrics that note improvement. For example, if a team is working on the benefits process that supports the 401(k) plan, the success of that process might be measured by how many employees participate in the plan. Therefore, improvements for the 401(k) process might prioritize those that most affect the participation rate.

You can also evaluate improvements in terms of their effect on the customer, which can include both internal and external customers.

Consider the Time and Resources Required

Assess the time and resources of each item and then section off those that are easy to complete as a group to execute first, so as to make the most initial progress with improvements with the least amount of resources. An underlying principle of continuous improvement is that changes should generally not require large amounts of capital in order to achieve improved results.

Step 3: Execute Your Action Plan

Once your team is clear about its top priorities, the team should then create action plans that will be executed in Step 3. Improvement initiatives require people to get clear about actions to take, such as:

- The sequence of the actions
- Who will be responsible for each action
- Who is responsible for ensuring all steps are completed

Make Sure Improvements Are Sustainable

A core concept for improvements is that they need to be sustainable over time. After all, good ideas that are not implemented or only exist for a matter of weeks would be a waste. Yet, the skills and strategy to maintain changes is quite challenging. When developing your action plan, there are many factors you need to consider, which not only address the change but also will ensure that your plan is sustainable. Process changes require stakeholders to "buy in" to the proposed changes, and you need to develop methods to monitor the change, to ensure accountability for the process owner and others.

Make Sure Stakeholders Buy into the Proposed Process Change

The topic of buy in and stakeholders is addressed in this phase of improvement. Buy in refers to how to ensure the action plan involves steps to explain the changes to the people who will be involved and to gain their cooperation. Many great improvements are lost due to the failure to obtain buy in on the change. It's difficult to just *mandate* new ways of doing things. People want to know how they would benefit from the change. They want to *feel included* in decisions that affect them.

Therefore, your action plans should include activities to *inform people* of changes or begin with *seeking feedback* before proceeding with important changes. Buy in refers to people directly impacted by proposed changes.

Develop Communication Plans with Stakeholders

Stakeholders refer to these same individuals, as well as anyone who has a vested interest in the change. Stakeholders may include vendors, owners, senior management, other functions that are impacted or who are affected to know about a change, or other employees anywhere in the organization who may be interested in the change.

Create Your Action Plans

Action plans contain specific actions to execute changes, but they also function as change management plans and communication plans to ensure that the change is well received, well executed, and also sustainable.

Step 4: Evaluate and Revise Your Plans

The final step of improvement involves evaluation and revision. Generally, improvement is a circular process that requires a team and the owner of the process to revisit their measurements and reconsider if the changes are actually effective.

Evaluate the Effects of the Actions Taken

How much time expires before a team evaluates the effects of their improvement-related changes varies by team. Some teams allow 90 days; others might allow 6 months or even a year. Generally, the team or other stakeholders might suggest changes or concerns over the original changes on an ongoing basis. The discipline of timing the evaluation and next round of changes also allows the original changes to solidify a bit, before considering further amendments.

Evaluation is an important tool in assessing the *sustainability of improvements* you've made to ensure they maintain the test of time. After all, why make changes if they disappear over time? Yet, sustainability requires a range of people management skills to successfully maintain the changes you make.

Evaluation involves not only checking metrics, but verifying how the changes you've made impacted the business in general, employees, customers, key metrics, and any other factor that merits review. Some evaluation is based on data. Other evaluation criteria can be obtained through observation or interviews.

Revise the Process to Make Additional Changes

Generally, the momentum of deciding to make changes and executing them is easier than the last part of the loop of evaluation and revision. The rewards are many for teams that keep to the discipline of evaluating their improvements and implementing additional changes or adjustments over time. Most core processes of HR could be redesigned several times before achieving higher success rates. Improvement is not a practice where only one attempt will realize significant results. Generally, what is put into the change process is what comes out of it. In other words, a few improvements lead to a small amount of change, whereas a great deal of improvement results in a great deal of change.

CHAPTER 5 SUMMARY

KEY IDEAS

- Three purposes are served by HR improving its own processes:
  1. Removing waste or steps that add no value
  2. Making employees happier and more productive
  3. Practicing the principles and methods

- Improving HR is completed through the following steps:
  1. Identifying opportunities
  2. Prioritizing opportunities
  3. Executing against action plans
  4. Reevaluating progress

- Improvement of HR is a multiyear process for even one thorough round of improvement. Progress requires clear prioritization of areas for opportunity over time.

STRATEGIC QUESTIONS FOR HR

1. Which HR processes most need to be evaluated for opportunity?
   _____
   _____
   _____
   _____
   _____
   _____
   _____

2. How do you currently hold your HR function accountable? _____
   _____
   _____
   _____
   _____
   _____
   _____

3. What are the opportunities for improving the HR function that link to visible metrics? _____

_____

_____

_____

_____

_____

_____

LEAN HR IMPLEMENTATION ACTIONS

1. Diagram all of your HR processes by title alone in a format that creates an overall employment cycle. Based on your current business strategy of your organization, which HR process might be best to impact your overall business or organizational strategy?

2. Which HR process most needs attention in your organization and why?

   ■ Create an improvement team to make measurable changes on one of your HR processes, including team members that perform work in the process, internal customers of the process, and others who can support needed changes.

   ■ Begin with gathering data and mapping the current situation.

   ■ Develop a list of improvement-related changes based on what is learned in the first step.

   ■ Execute an action plan of changes based on evaluating and prioritizing the opportunities, including creating a map for the future.

   ■ Make clear commitments to measure the process and evaluate changes in the future.

3. Actively seek out opportunities to study process mapping and process improvement, as this area has a strong link to improving HR programs and processes. Participate in many kinds of Lean training to become more familiar with how to use these tools for both HR processes and other needs that arise.

Chapter 6

Success through Powerful People Strategies

The last chapter described how HR needs to redesign each HR process to achieve more value. Apart from making sure every HR process adds value, this chapter shows how the relevance for key HR initiatives is gained when they link to an organization's current strategy. This chapter also covers how Lean business strategies, compared with traditional strategies, provide an even wider range of opportunities for HR to strengthen their overall relevance. Lastly, this chapter provides a new view for the HR department, where HR not only supports a business strategy, but can become strong enough to truly impact the direction of an organization and the achievement of key results.

To begin with, HR strategies and programs gain relevance when they are connected to achieving an organization's current business objectives or strategies. I have worked on an HR strategy that focused on supporting a business strategy to become the sole supplier to our large customers to dramatically increase sustainable revenue. Part of this effort involved having an interdepartmental team of people work together to drive customer-specific projects. The team created effective connections between several people within our organization who worked on various parts of the process for our customer and the corresponding people in our customer's organization, which we referred to as a "team-to-team link." HR participated in and facilitated some of the customer-related teams. Several months into the work, one

of the company's largest customers did make our company its sole supplier, which represented tens of millions of dollars of additional business.
This was an example of how a strategy to increase long-term revenue could
be fertile ground for HR to support the effort.

What is equally true is that HR programs tend to have considerably *less*
value when they are developed *apart* from business objectives. I have also
been part of HR strategies that have little relevance to business strategies,
even if they were well-meaning projects. For instance, I've helped create
leadership programs that have plenty of strong content but no direct link to
the current business goals, and hence they do little to help HR have strong
relevance to the current business objectives.

Therefore, this chapter considers the differences between traditional and
Lean business strategies, so as to provide a framework for understanding the
increased need for strengthening HR to achieve Lean strategies over more
traditional approaches.

How does a Lean business strategy provide tremendous opportunity for
HR to add value and be more relevant to an organization's success?

As HR becomes stronger with supporting Lean strategies, some might
see success as having HR objectives perfectly aligned with the business
objectives. However, perfect alignment is only one version of best practice. Consider whether HR can actually impact the business strategy with
such significance that it literally moves your business toward a direction
that your organization might not otherwise realize. Consider companies
that are considered best in class because of their people practices, such
as Toyota, or other popular examples, including GE, Southwest Airlines,
Microsoft, and 3M.

For example, Toyota was known to have clear people-related strategies for how people work, in terms of supporting the problem-solving
processes and reducing variations that involve people. Southwest has
a well-known approach to how to recruit and train its people to provide a certain flavor of customer service that keeps people flying on
Southwest. Microsoft has been noted as an organization that must effectively recruit the right kinds of talent to retain its market position. And
3M is an organization that made a people strategy for innovation part of
its overall success.

When could HR have so much impact that a business is truly more successful because of the efforts of the HR Department?

Traditional Business Strategies versus Lean or Continuous Improvement Business Strategies

A traditional business strategy frequently has a multifaceted approach to advance the position with customers, sales, and operations:

- The objectives often include clear goals of increasing and maintaining *customers*, while ensuring the customer base is a good fit for the organization's products or services.
- *Sales objectives* then link to customer objectives, which will have specific revenue and profitability goals and associated income.
- The *operational strategies* may focus on improving productivity or service levels to improve the profitability of the organization. These strategies also include intentions for advancing people and other support functions such as finance, information technologies, quality and human resources, to achieve the overarching strategies.

The overall objective is concentrated on improving results, as well as the long-term viability of the organization. Figures 6.1 and 6.2 compare the elements of a traditional business strategy with how these elements work together in a Lean business strategy.

As shown in Figure 6.1, Lean business strategies have generally the same elements as traditional strategies. Both contain a view of the customer, a sales and marketing approach, and an operational plan, with supporting strategies for people and other support functions. Yet the strategies diverge with the perspective on the customer, waste, and the role of people. Let's take a look at each of these differences.

Difference in Customer Perspective

Although the customer is *relevant* to a traditional strategy, customers are not nearly *the focal point*, as they are in Lean strategies. Best practices show that a strong orientation to all activities being done with the customer in mind is seen as optimal for an organization. This approach challenges traditional logic, which has the view that the primary purpose of an organization is to *be profitable* or *seek sustainability of its own interest*. In contrast, Lean principles are based on the belief that focusing on customer interests will, in the

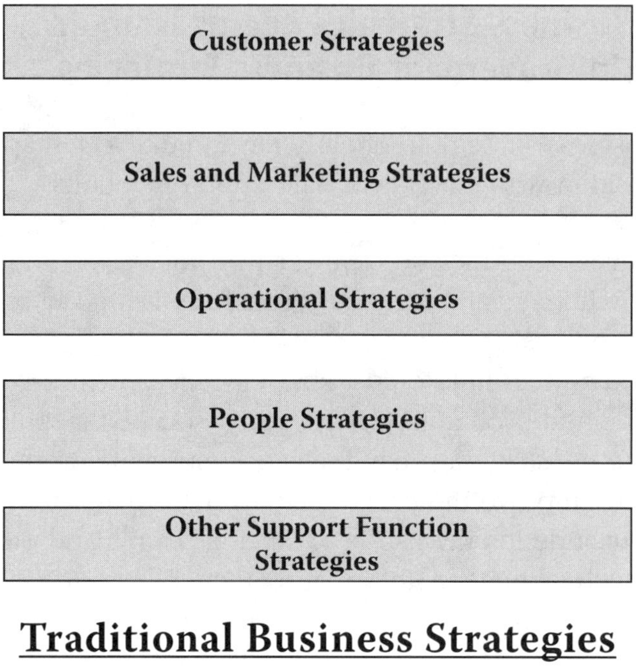

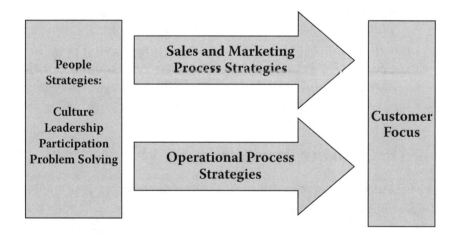

Traditional Business Strategies

Figure 6.1   Traditional business strategies.

Lean Business Strategies

Figure 6.2   Lean business strategies.

end, provide the best results for *both* the customer *and* the organization as a result. Said another way, profitability is a result of meeting customer needs, rather than being an overarching objective.

Difference in Workflows

The second difference is the view of streamlining workflows, because Lean strategies have a clear sense of *process and flow* across the business, with the satisfaction of customer needs as the end point or desired result. Lean strategies place heavy emphasis on cost reduction and quality improvement through leaning out the processes, in order to make the product correctly, with minimal errors and reducing costs. The process view found in Lean business strategies also creates more effective processes that cross over departmental lines by eliminating mishaps and gaps from the separations found in traditional "departmental silos." I have found communication gaps that are linked to many of the most significant problems in an organization are due to disconnects between departments. Lean strategies often change management roles to oversee processes instead of departments to support eliminating those gaps.

Difference in People Strategies

The *people strategies* are at the front of all Lean business strategies, and they drive each process in both the sales and operations areas. Therefore, people operate all core strategies—which makes people strategies a driving force behind the sales and operational strategies. Using the Lean principles mentioned in Chapter 1, the following is a list of features that are often seen in the development and execution of Lean business strategies. Lean business strategies commonly have:

- A primary focus on customer needs
- Significant improvements in key results
- A strategy that is developed and executed with involvement
- A need for process improvement
- A discipline about problem solving
- Visible communication of goals and ongoing results
- A variety of new leadership opportunities

HR Support of Business Strategy

The role of HR in supporting the attainment of key objectives is a core element of best practices. Therefore, your HR strategies need to be aligned within similar timeframes in accordance with how your organization's objectives are being supported. The link requires that each of your organizational objectives have some type of a people-related element that the HR function can support. The function supports the strategy by:

- Jobs that have the right components in them to achieve objectives
- Providing the right people
- Training people to support an initiative
- Ensuring the accountability systems are aligned with the strategy
- Rewarding or recognizing people who take part in the strategy

One example of supporting a business strategy through the people component was when I supported the implementation of a change in selling methods. Sales management wanted to increase the sales skills of its department to greatly enhance the revenue creation from more consultative sales approaches. I worked with the sales force to develop training, performance management, and recognition systems that supported this significant change in approach. The last HR strategy was to finally focus on the selection of candidates in the key sales positions to ensure that only people with the appropriate skills were hired.

Many believe the strongest vision of HR is that it would well support all strategies from a people point of view. Yes, potentially HR can actually *drive* the strategy and have an even greater impact on your organization as a whole. See the difference by comparing Figures 6.3 and 6.4.

Beyond Full Alignment

As a strategy driver, HR would seek opportunities to make people a core element of the business plan. Strategies may have a people element, but they often miss opportunities to really *capitalize* on what people offer. HR can help ensure business plans fully consider the potential of the people as a competitive advantage. As such, the people strategies that will be created by a more powerful HR department will not only impact results directly but can potentially change the *future* direction of an organization. Making

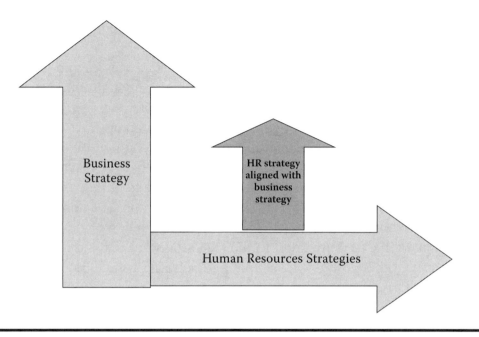

Figure 6.3   HR strategies that support by aligning with business strategy.

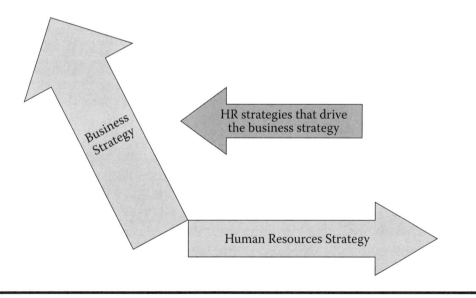

Figure 6.4   HR strategies that drive by impacting the business strategy.

people a strategic advantage is a key to being the best in the industry at anything.

However, change must be realized in a range of processes and practices before people practices would be considered strong enough to move a company to another level of success. This concept of creating enough real change to directly impact an organization is not just an abstract idea to me but has served as an ultimate goal in working to strengthen the role of HR in an organization. Ever since I first heard the idea that HR could truly drive a business strategy rather than just support it, I have kept that as the bar to be achieved in HR strategy and implementation. If more HR departments created higher expectations for their potential role, they would achieve more by not limiting their contribution to the background or playing purely a support role. Although it's obvious that people-related strategies can have a major impact on an organization's success, it's been much less obvious that the department devoted to people can have a major impact on an organization's success as well.

CHAPTER 6 SUMMARY

KEY IDEAS

- HR strategies need to link to your organization's overall business strategy.
- HR Lean efforts can begin in several places in your business, including the sales and marketing, operations, or service centers or in the various support functions, such as quality or finance.
- Lean business strategies compared to traditional business strategies naturally provide more opportunity for HR to add value by supporting or driving Lean strategic efforts.
- Because Lean strategies begin with people-related strategies, HR has a key role in developing those strategies and ensuring they flow through both sales and operational processes, with the internal and external customers in mind.
- As HR continues to evolve, a new vision of having HR truly impact the direction of an organization and the results it achieves will not only be possible; it will also be an option organizations may elect to pursue.

STRATEGIC QUESTIONS FOR HR

1. What are possible entry points for you to develop an HR continuous improvement strategy around your organization's business strategy? Consider whether there are opportunities in the sales effort, the operational or service aspect of your business, or if any of the support functions most need HR support.

_____

_____

_____

_____

_____

_____

_____

_____

_____

2. What is the belief system of key leaders in your organization around continuous improvement or other types of Lean concepts? Reflect on conversations with key leaders about their experiences and current ideas about how continuous improvement can be used in the workplace. _____

_____

_____

_____

_____

_____

_____

_____

3. How could HR *drive* your business strategy rather than simply *support* it? How could expanding your ideas about the power of HR help your business move forward or achieve new levels of success? _____

_____

_____

_____

_____
_____
_____
_____

LEAN HR IMPLEMENTATION ACTIONS

1. Review your organization's current business strategy and look for links to continuous improvement or Lean principles.
   - Seek out the comprehensive versions of your organizational strategy.
   - Meet with people at a senior level to discuss the overall strategies.
   - Based on a thorough understanding of your strategy, explore areas where HR programs (recruitment strategies, training needs, performance management systems, recognition and rewards) could build momentum.
   - Have exploratory conversations with key leaders about their portion of the overall strategy, and suggest ways HR could help them achieve their objectives. Once you identify ways that the key leader would support HR interventions, seek to reach agreement about HR efforts that will be executed on their behalf.

2. What connections or disconnections are there in your current HR initiatives to your current business strategy?
   - Evaluate your current HR initiatives against the business strategies just reviewed. _____
   _____
   _____
   _____
   _____
   _____
   _____
   - Where do you see strong alignment? _____
   _____
   _____

_____

_____

_____

_____

_____

■ Where do you see a neutral effect of the HR initiative on the business strategy? _____

_____

_____

_____

_____

_____

_____

_____

■ Where do you see actual disconnects or conflicts in current HR initiatives and your business strategy? _____

_____

_____

_____

_____

_____

_____

_____

■ Are there compelling reasons to keep any key HR initiative that is neutral or having a negative impact on current strategic initiatives? _____

_____

_____

_____

_____

_____

_____

_____

3. Actively seek out information on current thinking about Lean or continuous improvement principles, because HR business consulting is greatly strengthened by knowledge of Lean and continuous improvement principles.
   - Review written materials or books that provide either overviews of Lean ideas and methods or provide in-depth information on specific areas of Lean.
   - Participate in as many kinds of Lean training as you can locate to become more familiar with training needs for improved results with various employee groups.

HOW HR CAN INFLUENCE AND CHANGE WORK CULTURES

III

Section II focused on how strengthening the HR department addresses a primary root cause of failed improvement attempts as well as attempts to more fully utilize talent. This section covers several aspects of cultural change that require HR's involvement to support and sustain.

Chapter 7 considers how cultural objectives based on the business strategy need to be developed into daily behaviors, with an emphasis on the underlying values to help promote those behaviors. Affecting daily behaviors and attitudes requires the use of any and all methods to promote consistent messages, which begins to be understood better in Chapter 8, with the role of HR in developing strong cultures.

Strengthening a culture also requires diligence, if not vigilance, to remove messages that conflict with or detract from key cultural or strategic messages. Chapter 9 deals with how a range of activities in the workplace that are often overlooked affects behaviors and messages, and sends powerful messages to people about what matters or is important. These can be doing a considerable amount of damage, and there is often no real awareness of the issues. Any change process needs to be measured.

Finally in Section III, Chapter 10 reviews the use of surveys as a powerful tool to measure culture, employee satisfaction, or customer issues.

Chapter 7

Changing Employee Attitudes and Daily Behaviors

In the last chapter, we discussed how Lean HR can help you develop and implement your organization's business strategies and the corresponding people strategies. This chapter provides a framework for helping you develop and implement a desired *culture* for your organization, which is one of the most powerful ways HR can support an organization's business objectives. Part of what makes culture a powerful place for HR to contribute to the organization's success is that it is rooted in the organization's values, which are based on the emotional energies of your people, which drive behaviors whether they be success-oriented or not. This chapter describes both a continuous improvement culture and a general approach for customizing cultural elements against your organization's long-term objectives.

The Role of Organizational Culture in Achieving Success

What Is Culture?

Although *culture* is a common term, it is exceedingly challenging to define the real nature of what it encompasses. In general, *culture refers to patterns of behaviors and attitudes.* Therefore, designing and implementing a culture establishes what patterns of behaviors and attitudes will help an organization achieve their strategic objectives. This chapter ends with a look at how the work of changing your culture can influence those who might be open to changing their beliefs and patterns of behavior, but require interventions to affect them. The role of HR is to help set a course to develop a Lean culture (or any desired culture) by ensuring that identified beliefs and behaviors are reflected in all matters related to employment.

What is the potential value in changing or affecting the patterns of behaviors and attitudes in your organization?

Every Organization Has a Culture

Every organization has a culture—even if there is not a clear strategy to foster a particular culture. Many organizations may not typically assess their culture, much less design a culture of choice. Yet even without any specific intent, a culture forms when a group of people work together, create patterns of behaviors, and develop trends of commonly held ideas or attitudes.

For example, I've worked in an organization that focused on customer service and having premium products. The organization then focused on these two issues in a range of ways that showed up in daily life. We worked on internal customer satisfaction as a way to solve problems. We publicized concerns about customers in a way that expressed an attitude of importance and urgency. People commonly mentioned customers in their conversation as a reason why something was happening. It didn't matter which part of the business someone worked in, the issue of delivering premium products to our customers was always a part of the work. Therefore, I would describe our culture as having a strong element of customer focus—not because it was in a strategic document, but because *customer focus was part of how we talked and worked, every day.*

What are the values likely expressed on a daily basis that drive the results in an organization? Is independence valued? How are new ideas treated? What about people who change or at least question prior ways of doing things? What is the pace of the organization in terms of daily life? In an organization that helps surface ideas and innovation, there certainly are daily patterns of behaviors that help drive its success. This chapter considers whether those patterns can be strengthened for greater success. Because culture is so pervasive in a day's activities, it's like the air in the room.

Yet it is still commonly understood that designing a culture is an opportunity any organization may leverage to gain additional advantage in improving organizational performance. The desire to foster a culture leads to the need to develop cultural objectives that support desired behaviors that bring targeted results.

Setting Cultural Objectives for Your Organization

The term *cultural objectives* is not common, but for our purposes, we will refer to *strategic* objectives that are *cultural* in nature. Whereas business plans are often on an 18-month basis as well as a 5-year basis, culture and an organization's underlying values have a much longer-term horizon than business plans or strategies, of approximately 10 years or more. In other words, a culture is something that evolves over time.

Therefore, cultural objectives would be goals for creating patterns of behavior that support strategies, but exist well beyond their time horizon. Patterns of behavior that might be of interest would be how people interact as teams, create new ways of doing things, make decisions that are good for customers, go the extra mile for customer satisfaction, or how people focus on quality work in all they do. The designation of cultural objectives is one way to help an organization achieve success by becoming clear about what desired behaviors and attitudes need to be strengthened to heighten success.

Cultural objectives will clearly have time horizons for implementation or changes, but they would generally not have an end in sight after changes take place. This book refers to cultural objectives as separate from business objectives, because they are often looked at separately. This chapter reviews the common elements of a continuous improvement culture, to reflect how organizations with an appropriately linked strategy might direct a culture change to achieve enhanced results.

Identifying Your Organization's Cultural Values

Cultural objectives focus on the strategies for implementing behaviors. Values are the component of culture that relates to the *underlying assumptions that guide daily behavior.* Values create codes of conduct and common attitudes, and yet are based upon the emotional significance to people, which is often what most powerfully drives behavior. Values represent what is important to an organization, which then becomes what's normal in people's attitudes. Helping to align people with values can help create engagement when someone personally shares or is aligned to a stated value.

Another way to look at cultural values is to compare them to elements of branding products. Branding focuses on particular concepts that are communicated in such a manner that develops a perception or a feeling, even though it may not be conscious. Branding allows consumers to align with

Table 7.1 Potential Values and Related Lean Principles

Value	Related Lean Principle
Customer first	Customer focus
Excellence	Continuous improvement
Initiative	Participation
Sustainability	Process management
Accountability	Problem solving
Transparency	Visual measurements
Equality	Visionary leadership

brand concepts and thus buy a product or service. In a manner similar to branding, HR can communicate values that are the essence of Lean cultural elements, which people then buy into, and this generates momentum to permeate the culture. Table 7.1 shows how the seven Common Lean Principles can be reflected in values and the emotional essence of the value.

Key Concepts of Continuous Improvement Cultures

For organizations that desire or already have a specific strategy to use Lean principles, the following cultural elements reflect how to implement them as patterns of behaviors and attitudes or a work culture. These concepts are not intended to be an inclusive outline of a continuous improvement culture, but they provide some common characteristics as an indication of how these cultures are designed. Although continuous improvement is often associated with a particular management practice or process to evaluate systems for opportunities for better performance, a continuous improvement culture takes this practice well beyond a set of steps or a process and makes it a pervasive *standard* of behavior. Specifically, continuous improvement cultures include these common elements:

1. Customer focus
2. Continuous improvement
3. Broad participation
4. Process management
5. Team-based factual problem solving

6. Visual measurements

7. Visionary leadership

Each element is described in the rest of this chapter, beginning with customer focus, because all things in Lean or continuous improvement begin and end with the customer in mind.

Cultural Element Number 1: Customer Focus

Corporations can be enhanced by developing a strong orientation to customer needs; there's an obvious benefit to ensuring that a business stays relevant to the customer base, based on real needs being met over time. Organizations with a strong customer focus are often "customer centric" in their approach to providing products and services—making the customer the center of all strategies.

In terms of attitude, these organizations value *customer sacredness* and put the customer first as a matter of priority, with an emotional essence that reflects reverence, respect, and urgency. Customers detect when their interests are treated with a high degree of urgency. Valuing customer sacredness therefore protects and potentially increases revenue. For example, think of a time you went to a store that clearly seemed to value your business and treat your concerns with a sense of urgency and respect, and then think of a store that didn't. Which one did you want to go back to?

HR is able to support these efforts by building these behaviors and attitudes into jobs (which likely affects job content, training, performance management, and potentially rewards). HR also builds policies and practices that strengthen customer satisfaction by ensuring employees understand customer needs. An example would be developing job content that illuminates customer focus and a sense of urgency in daily work for the benefit of the customers. HR would then drive this cultural element or value into selection, training, accountability, and recognition.

Cultural Element Number 2: Continuous Improvement

If customers are the focus or purpose of work, doing a better job serving customers or the "pursuit of excellence" is the foundation of the next hallmark of a continuous improvement culture. As a pervasive behavioral standard, this is well beyond a distinct program or recognizable process. Beyond identified objectives, the need for ongoing evaluation and change to advance improved performance becomes integrated into most work processes.

As an attitude, continuous improvement values *excellence*. A sense of quality and high standards is supported by emotional qualities of idealism, ambition, and purpose. People from these organizations regularly speak to how they are getting better in each of their processes as a normal part of their day. Excellence demands people not be satisfied at maintenance and that they have a penchant for superior performance. Improvement efforts of a wide variety will be found throughout the organization and are required to be part of most managers' work.

Because the requirements for improvement are often widespread, HR can have a significant role in supporting behaviors and skills that drive continuous improvement as well as building it into all job content. As just described in the previous section on customer focus, job content for continuous improvement with a value on excellence can affect each of the core HR programs as well as a range of policies and practices.

For example, I've seen the requirement of demonstrated improvement built into job requirements to hire new managers. I've built continuous improvement skills into HR training programs that help people learn more about how to achieve improved performance. I've developed accountability systems that clearly require improved performance over time in all facets of the performance of a job.

Excellence in all aspects of an organization's function certainly requires everyone to be involved, which leads us to the next element, *broad participation*.

Cultural Element Number 3: Broad Participation

These organizations often involve a significant amount of participation by people throughout the organization. The underlying belief of a continuous improvement culture is that all work is improved if completed with:

- Significant input from a range of people that are involved
- A deeper understanding of issues involved
- Greater engagement with needed changes
- Implementation by and through groups of people instead of individuals

The emotional content of participation is linked to trust, safety, and willingness. The passion that people bring into the workplace has much to do with whether they trust the people around them, which makes them willing to take initiative. Long-term success requires that people care about their work, and this is supported by creating an environment of trust and safety.

Organizations that value participation as part of their culture will easily point to improvements that have come from people in a wide variety of roles. For example, I recently visited an organization that had many books containing lists of ideas that had been generated by employees and successfully implemented. These efforts go well beyond employee suggestion programs and use distinct participation processes to create meaningful engagement—of which many require HR design and support.

Cultural Element Number 4: Process Management

If all roads (and hence processes) lead to customers, and continued improvement is required, it becomes clear how process management supports the pursuit of excellence for the good of the customers. Process management refers to the fact that all businesses are a series of processes that link together to provide a product or service to its customers. The process orientation allows people to break down the components of a business into segments that can be redesigned for improvement and ensure value is added at each step along the way. Generally, businesses involved in continuous improvement will have physically mapped out the majority of their organization's processes and redesigned the processes for greater efficiency and service to the customers.

As an attitude, these organizations value sustainability that is emotionally grounded in discipline from repeating a best practice or gold standard. Sustainability as a value is linked to ensuring that what generates the target must be repeated and what moves away from the target is removed or altered. As an attitude, there is an absence of reactive emotions such as anger and blame. Sustainability is rooted in ensuring that people are trained and held accountable to a standard over time. Management has the key responsibility for ensuring that work standards are well developed and well understood to build the most success.

People I've spoken to who have cultures with a strong process orientation generally link problems to the need for process changes instead of "who to blame." HR may then be involved in supporting a culture of process orientation by building aspects of process management into management roles and aspects of problem solving on a process basis into most jobs, which replaces focusing on "who did it." HR might then need to provide process management training to support these job requirements to help build those skills into the workforce. Once process management is part of the work, accountability and recognition systems will likely refer to process and improvement as well.

Cultural Element Number 5: Team-Based Factual Problem Solving

Solving problems is a day-to-day activity in almost any organization. Problems are a normal part of work. What makes problem solving an element of continuous improvement cultures is the focus on a distinct methodology to be applied to the majority of any significant issues and the practice of solving, often by teams. Many organizations suffer through a range of problems on a daily basis with little idea of how to resolve them. In contrast, continuous cultures are committed to addressing problems in a manner that is based on facts and through teamwork to ensure that performance is improved over time as difficult problems are solved efficiently and effectively.

The attitudes linked to this type of problem-solving focus on *accountability* to solve problems, not *blaming* people for when things go wrong. Defects and problems are naturally demotivating, so these cultures find energy and motivation by fixing problems as they move forward. *Accountability* is very different from *blame* because it focuses on how job content, specification, and standards create a result. When the result is unacceptable, you should then review the process, not the intention of the people who are working the process. Examination of people in the process is more about how their work is structured, trained, and monitored than whether they intentionally deliver problems.

HR would then be critical in guiding managers to involve the assessment of people against effective problem solving, instead of making it constantly a matter of discipline, which is closely linked to blaming people. Problem solving requires a wide range of skill building, including developing the methods as well as facilitating team processes to address issues. These same teams are continually linking problem solving with the improvement of visible measured results.

When I'm in an organization that has a culture of team-based factual problem solving, I typically see evidence of teams working together on important issues and the gathering of data to better understand problems as well. Managers will excitedly speak about problems that are being studied and understood, and they proudly point to the many team members who were involved in getting to new levels of performance. HR can have an enormous role in building problem solving into job specifications, development programs, accountability, and recognition systems.

Cultural Element Number 6: Visual Measurement of Results

Results are visibly measured in these cultures as a reinforcement to drive behaviors that are achievement focused. Continual improvement requires that results be fueled by the majority of people being focused on key objectives, how they are being measured, and regularly monitoring for improvement.

The attitude linked to visual measurements is transparency as an organizational value, and it is demonstrated as willingness (if not a propensity) to release information to everyone about all key measurements. The emotional links for transparency are knowledge and empowerment. The benefit of this approach to working with people is that if they have the facts and feel knowledgeable they are able to deal more effectively with the range of issues related to running a business.

Some cultures make this a game-like environment where the "scoreboard" is highly visibly and has broad meaning to those in the organization. The scoreboard mentality in a workplace often links to a sense of fun and excitement that connects with improvement. The visual results are best if they are based on the "line of sight," or where the employee works, to ensure the measurements motivate employees. In contrast, some posted measurements apply to everyone in a facility, but have little meaning to individuals about the relative success of their personal or team's work results.

HR is positioned to be well able to help champion visible metrics and ensure people both understand and are motivated by knowing how they are performing against visible goals and supporting the celebrations with each success.

Cultural Element Number 7: Inspirational Leadership

Leadership in a continuous improvement culture takes on a much more elevated role because it is the role of bringing people's abilities to life. Inspirational leaders are not necessarily leaders who know the most or who are the best people in terms of their skills and abilities; instead, inspirational leaders are those who *bring out the best* in all the people in their organization. Inspirational leaders do a better job accessing the talents of people they manage or lead, so that they can provide a larger benefit to the organization.

The organizational value of equality of its people supports inspirational leadership and is founded in the idea that people are truly equals. In contrast, many workplaces reinforce the idea that people are in *a hierarchy of value*. Terms like "reporting up" and people "on top" reflect values that management is somehow higher (in other words, better) than others who are "below" them.

The link between inspirational leadership and Lean strategies is that inspirational leaders help people to understand the whole process of the work they do, to solve problems together in teams, and to always keep the customer in mind. These are individuals who lead by *coaching* instead of *telling*. They have a firm way of supporting their groups and holding them accountable, but they allow people to flourish freely. HR has a significant role in designing leadership roles or job descriptions that require this type of leadership, which *grows capabilities* instead of *governing people.*

Now that we have covered the elements of establishing a generic culture as well as the values and emotions linked to a Lean culture, we move on to the next chapter on creating culture change. Chapter 8 will discuss considerations on working with employees who naturally are in favor of desired culture changes, and how to not overly invest time in people who resist the changes.

CHAPTER 7 SUMMARY

KEY IDEAS

- Your organization's business strategy drives your culture.
- All businesses have a culture, but intentional implementation of a culture strengthens your ability to achieve results under a broader range of conditions.
- Each Lean principle can be translated to a Lean cultural element, with an underlying Lean value that provides the emotional essence or Lean attitudes that build Lean behaviors.

STRATEGIC QUESTIONS FOR HR

1. What are the elements of your culture?

_____
_____
_____

2. How do the elements of your culture compare to a Lean culture?

_____
_____
_____

3. What is HR's role in developing your organizational culture?

_____
_____
_____

LEAN HR IMPLEMENTATION ACTIONS

1. If your organization does not have a clearly articulated culture, draft a customized approach for your culture that fits your particular business.
   - Begin with gathering strategic documents that outline either the business strategy or might be restricted to a segment of the business (such as a department or division).
   - For each strategic objective, list elements that have cultural implications. Cultural implications are common behaviors that support the attainment of the objectives. _____

   _____
   _____
   _____
   _____
   _____
   _____

   - Once you have a list of cultural objectives that are developed from your strategy, draft them in language that would be readily recognized in your environment. _____

   _____
   _____

_____

_____

_____

■ Either in individual meetings or in a group setting, validate your ideas for cultural objectives through members
of senior management who are responsible for the overall
strategy.

■ Draft a document describing the cultural element that can be
readily referenced not only by those in HR but also others in
leadership roles for use in evaluating how the desired culture
is or is not being supported.

■ Implement agreed upon cultural elements into all practices,
policies, and HR programs (which will be described in detail
throughout this book).

2. For each Lean culture element, list ways (or groups) in which
you see this element reflected in your organization. Do you see
these elements in the HR programs?

■ Customer focus:

_____

_____

_____

_____

_____

■ Continuous Improvement:

_____

_____

_____

_____

_____

■ Broad participation:

_____

_____

_____

_____

_____

■ Process management:

_____

_____

_____

_____

_____

■ Problem solving:

_____

_____

_____

_____

_____

■ Visual measurement:

_____

_____

_____

_____

_____

■ Inspirational leadership:

_____

_____

_____

_____

_____

FOR EACH LEAN CULTURE ELEMENT

■ List ways (or groups) in which you see this element reflected in your organization.
■ Describe the attitudes do you see expressed.
■ Describe the emotions that are linked to these attitudes and elements. How are the emotions important in terms of creating positive energy for success?
■ Do you see these elements in the HR programs?

Chapter 8

Lessons on Culture Implementations for Lean HR

Chapter 7 focused on cultures in general and detailed a culture that supports Lean strategies or Lean principles; this chapter begins by describing how to implement a culture by first ensuring that any approach is customized to a particular organization. Next, the role of HR in implementing culture is highlighted. The chapter ends with a discussion of how to identify which individuals are in alignment, are neutral, or disagree with the overall culture, and shows how to use this information to support a culture initiative.

A General Approach to Designing a Culture

Chapter 7 covered some basic ideas about culture and how these relate to Lean principles; however, actual cultural descriptions would not likely ever match something written in a book. Like a fingerprint, each organization has its own particular culture, and our work in Lean HR is to help uncover what is there and create intentionality about what can be implemented. The future intention begins with an organization's strategy: it can be determined what culture or patterns of behavior would be required to drive success.

For example, if an organization's strategy is to be the leading innovator in its area of products, then the culture would be designed to ensure that common behaviors of *creativity* and *innovation* are prevalent. A strong link between a strategy and a culture helps ensure success, through driving more of the behaviors that implement the strategy more fully.

An example of this that I always remember is working in an organization that wanted to change people's view of quality. The business strategy was to more solidly position the product line as premium quality, and we wanted to be able to feature how our organization created a truly premium product. We had a cultural objective to bring more quality-related behaviors into all our processes and have a pervading attitude about quality. What I saw as we changed was that people more commonly referred to quality when talking to anyone, including customers.

We also changed who handled quality to the people who made the product, instead of having a separate "quality assurance" or "quality control" department. This required a lot more people to know how to do quality checks and to know more about our quality standards. We had a range of training events that taught people about what practices led to higher levels of quality, which led to more and more people talking about quality and making changes to improve the quality of our products as well as the services that supported them. Within a year, quality had improved and we had begun to think of ourselves as a "quality-centric" organization.

Many businesses have behaviors they want to target to achieve goals. As a business lays out a set of strategies to drive its future directly, it's important to ask: *What do our people need to do well to achieve our strategies?*

Customize a Plan to Implement a Culture

It is important that each organization — that is, *your* organization—customize the work in this area. Although the ideas about Lean culture based on Lean principles covered in Chapter 7 presents some common ideas and language found in Lean organizations, no two organizations do this in the same way. This allows an organization to internalize the work and not take on some identity from the outside. Therefore, it is critical that the work be done in a manner that is true for your specific organization. Language or terms need to be typical to your organization so that they can be integrated most easily into the daily conversation of your employees. For example, I have been in companies that refer to their culture in terms like "Seven Features of Business Excellence" or the "Five Pillars of Success." What is important is that you work with what is currently in place. The models are meant to provide a framework for understanding how elements work together, which you then need to customize to the needs of your particular organization.

Continuous improvement includes an underlying premise to optimize people's talents and abilities, which eliminates one of the greatest sources of waste in an organization. The definition of a continuous improvement culture is expanded to specific key concepts. Section IV of the book (Chapters 11 to 14) demonstrate how these concepts inform HR processes.

HR's Critical Role with Cultural Objectives

As your organization gains clarity about the values, behaviors, and attitudes that are required to achieve strategic objectives, it becomes evident that HR is the owner of many processes that support them. The purpose of this material from an HR perspective is that desired cultural elements become the foundation for a range of HR activities:

■ First, the desired cultural elements may drive the formulation of desired competencies or behaviors within jobs. For example, if innovation is a critical element of a newly developed business strategy and the culture, jobs may need to be redesigned, with new requirements for demonstrating innovativeness in various aspects of the work.

■ Second, these cultural elements will then be applied to core HR programs, including selection, training, performance management, and rewards. Using our example above of driving innovation, approaches to selection may need to be added that validate a person's inclination towards innovation. Training may be required that builds creativity skills and processes for handling innovation in the workplace. Performance management systems may need to be revised to ensure accountabilities are in place for innovation within certain jobs. Rewards that recognize innovation may need to be put in place.

■ Last, most HR policies, practices, and norms should be affected by desired cultural elements. Again, using our example, HR needs to be alert to any needed changes to policies and practices to reinforce the desire for innovation. Putting in a new practice of employee suggestions with an emphasis on innovation will help reinforce the need for innovation by everyone.

Figure 8.1 provides a view of how Lean cultural elements come from the strategy and depicts how these elements are then used to inform HR policies, practices, and programs for a robust implementation that surely impacts results.

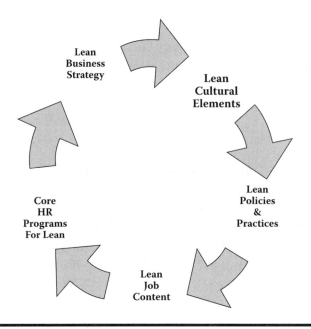

Figure 8.1   Lean HR for continuous improvement.

HR Helps Differentiate the Effect Individuals Have on Culture

When implementing a change to a culture, it is critical to gain awareness of which individuals in a group or throughout the organization strongly agree with it, which disagree, and which are more neutral toward the elements. The purpose in understanding individual attitudes is to focus efforts on those individuals most likely to be influenced towards alignment with the change. Because the efforts to achieve alignment with those who have positive agreement is the focus, an organization would do well to choose carefully how to handle disagreement. The reason to be careful is that those who disagree loudly often attract everyone's attention and concern. I've seen people commonly insist that everyone agree and "get on board."

For example, one of my first change efforts in a facility involved getting people to handle their shift changes a certain way. A few people complained loudly that the new procedures weren't fair and caused them to do work they hadn't done before. I spent so much time worrying about the two people who objected that the 60 other people who were looking to me for direction were left waiting for my attention. It was an important lesson that it was the majority who needed to get in alignment, and I needed to allow the few people time to get over their concerns. I needed to focus on making sure those who were simply waiting for a clear vision and a chance to move forward were not left hanging because of a few loud objectors. Let's look at each type of individual.

Dealing with Individuals Who Are Strongly Aligned to a Lean Culture

Individuals with a strong alignment to a Lean culture will display an ease with participation, involvement, leadership opportunities, collaboration, and fact-based problem solving. When I meet these people, they are often excited about the teams they are leading, the people they are helping to find new talents in themselves, and the teamwork they are enjoying while solving nagging problems. These individuals are slow to blame people and quick to look at the underlying processes. The value of these individuals to the business is that these employees can lead the way for those who are unsure of the value of these principles to the organization.

Dealing with Individuals Who Strongly Disagree with a Lean Culture

Individuals with strong disagreement with Lean principles will be easy to locate, because they are often vocal about their disagreement. These individuals may disagree and seek to establish forms of informal and formal leadership. If they are not in supervisory roles, they may be challenging to Lean ideas because they don't think the ideas work, or that they require extra work and can threaten their future employment.

If they have supervisory responsibilities, they are often overly invested in the traditional hierarchal ideals of a few people being in charge who have superior abilities to the others and who must be allowed to be "in charge" to get the desired results. These individuals will also typically have a view of accountability that includes a strong link to the use of *discipline* to achieve results. Rather than seeing success as something to *motivate towards*, these individuals instead see what *negative consequence* will fall to those who fail to perform. Unfortunately, these individuals often find team problem solving as a team to be a waste of time, and they seek to resolve issues by determining who is to blame and then dishing out the consequences. The problem for the business is that this leadership style squelches others who seek to permanently solve problems.

These individuals can become the focus of efforts at changing an organization's culture because of the assumption that changing their views is essential. In the long run, Lean changes can involve removing some of these individuals from the organization or from leadership roles, although it is often unnecessary to make this the focus initially.

Dealing with People in Neither Group

Much would be lost if the focus is on those individuals who disagree with Lean principles; the real challenge in a culture initiative is focusing on those *in the middle* who can be swayed to the positive side—of agreeing with Lean principles. Roughly 70 to 80% of people are typically strongly for or against a particular set of cultural elements or values. Those in the middle are able to be influenced to be in strong alignment. Efforts to influence those people in the middle can take many forms, including a range of verbal and written communications aimed at groups or individuals.

I've used meetings most often with groups, which are then supported with written documents for those people who need to read what's being said. A blend of larger meetings mixed with either small group or individual meetings may be necessary when the issues are more complex and a range of concerns need to be addressed. I often remind managers that change happens one person at a time, so communication needs to be developed with that in mind. Each person has his or her own response to a situation, and the more you need that person's individual support, the more you need to work through his or her concerns with that person, individually.

For example, I had a situation where we wanted to have the supervisors of our facility work more as coaches than supervisors. As we communicated this change to the entire group, most people had a number of questions about how it would work, what would be different, and what could go wrong. As we met with people in groups and individually, we understood better the issues that needed attention, and we were able to more fully implement the original plan to change our culture of top-down management to a team environment. In the end, many of the individuals all influenced the work through our efforts to listen to them one at a time and to take their perspective into account in our plans going forward.

This chapter reviewed the role of HR in implementing a change in culture, including developing a customized approach to supporting this type of effort. The next chapter looks at the role HR needs to play in ensuring that desired cultural elements are reflected in policies and practices.

CHAPTER 8 SUMMARY

KEY IDEAS

Customizing your approach to Lean HR requires that it fit your unique business and your current strategy (or strategies) and that you utilize vocabulary that will be recognized in your environment.

STRATEGIC QUESTIONS FOR HR

■ What are the elements of your culture?

_____
_____
_____
_____

■ What is HR's role in developing your organizational culture?

_____
_____
_____
_____

■ What is the focus of your culture efforts in terms of individuals in the organization?

_____
_____
_____
_____

■ What is the impact of individuals who strongly disagree with your culture? Does this need attention?

_____
_____
_____
_____

LEAN HR IMPLEMENTATION ACTIONS

1. Review the impact of people who are strongly for or against a desired culture.
   ■ List individuals who are known to be clearly in favor of the culture and those who are against the culture. _____
   _____

_____

_____

_____

- List the impact of both groups on the environment and the success of the culture._____

_____

_____

_____

_____

2. Now that you've considered the impact the various groups have on the success or failure of your strategic cultural objectives, develop action plans for each group. Begin with generating ideas of what types of activities will help you best leverage the strengths of those in alignment, put most of the effort to those who are neutral, and pay less attention to those in disagreement. While those in disagreement should not allowed to be focal point, it's critical at times that disagreement be directly dealt with in an effective manner.

   - For the group that naturally aligns with a Lean culture, describe action plans that utilize the strengths of these group members, such as having them help with communication efforts, teaching classes, and helping with other design and implementation activities.

   - Next, develop action plans for those against the culture that seek to at least address their concerns and may need to address possible reduction of their roles if they are in key leadership positions.

   - Last, develop action plans for those who are neutral or waiting to decide that optimize the likelihood of impacting them, which might include communications efforts, benchmarking trips, and customer visits.

Chapter 9

Policies, Communications, and Celebrations Need to Reflect Your Organization's Values

Many people believe that the policies in the employee handbook have little or no effect on results. However, it is true that handbooks, written communications, and other common practices *do* have an effect on results through the significant messages they send about "what is important."

For example, consider how employees receive conflicting messages when they attend some type of improvement training or activity, and then come to find their normal work plan unchanged. Employees may be *told* that your organization values specific concepts, but they may find that the policies in the handbook are quite different. These disconnects go unnoticed by many people because they are part of the everyday landscape of typical workplaces. However, although they go unnoticed, such conflicting messages detract from efforts to change culture, and more important, they create the perception of a lack of integrity on the part of the organization's leadership. HR has an important role to play in ensuring that your organization's policies and practices are aligned with its intended messages and that they protect the integrity of your leaders.

Many of the topics presented in this chapter are not often included in plans for culture change, including handbook policies, communications, celebrations, safety practices, physical environments, and strategic planning. However, these topics are, in fact, areas of opportunity to convey consistent messages—or, more important, they can be potential obstacles that prevent meaningful change. Lean principles have a distinct approach to these topics that involves creating psychological safety, blurring the lines between management and nonmanagement, as well as reducing the need to control people in the workplace.

Assess Your Organization's Policies against Lean Principles

To develop consistent cultural messages, evaluate each policy against your organization's cultural objectives. Often, there might be disconnects between the messages people are given when they are working on a continuous improvement team and how they are treated if they are tardy or make a mistake. Therefore, you need to assess your organization's policies to determine whether they have a positive effect, a negative effect, or are neutral to key messages.

Table 9.1 depicts how this audit might look for an evaluation of common policies and how they either support or detract from the Lean cultural elements reviewed in the last chapter, and thus impact a Lean culture. Next we will review these ratings and consider what might need to be done where there are obvious opportunities.

Protect Employees' Psychological Safety

In my experience, the greatest disconnect between what companies say and what they do is the area of discipline. Table 9.1 shows discipline as an

Table 9.1   Conduct a Policy Audit against Continuous Improvement Culture

Policy Description	Reinforces the Culture	Has a Negligible Effect on the Culture	Negatively Impacts the Culture
Discipline	Opportunity		Problem
Tardiness	Opportunity		Problem
Attendance	Opportunity		Problem
Benefits		No change	
Conduct		No change	

Note: See sections on psychological safety, blurring the lines between employees and accountability versus control to create new ideas about how these policies might change.

opportunity in terms of its effect on Lean cultural elements. Many organizations seek to communicate that solving problems is good, finding the root cause of a problem is good, and understanding how to fix the process is good, but in practice if people make mistakes they are punished or "written up." I have met with employees who are confused and angry that they have just been taught in a training class that problems should be uncovered to be solved for the future and then have been written up or seen someone else written up that same week for a problem in the work.

For example, I was working in HR initially when a major cultural change was made regarding how discipline was handled in a facility. Managers kept viewing the pull back on discipline as "soft" or "weak." The key understanding of what it meant to manage was to ensure people were *held accountable* through *discipline.* Yet I had already learned enough about process management, problem solving, and participation to know that anything that would cause employees to retreat and withdraw could not be good for the work that really needed to be done to create great processes that took meeting customer needs to new levels. Creating psychological safety became an important aspect of creating a culture suitable for attaining meaningful improved results. Discipline was a key enemy of psychological safety and had to be revised to move forward. However, getting managers to understand why was a significant challenge.

However, there are organizations that link the way mistakes are treated to supporting the learning process, which is critical to creating psychological safety for employees. It was a shock the first time I observed an organization that had overhauled its discipline system. We were on a benchmarking visit as we developed a skill-based pay plan and needed to see an example of this pay structure. The company had the foresight to cross-train all employees to strengthen skills, and also involved them all in problem solving and process improvement. This same group had removed any type of discipline that would interfere with creating engaged employees who helped identify problems and then worked together to solve them. They wanted highly motivated team players to make their products, which resulted in the need for fewer employees to get more product of higher quality made. This first experience of witnessing a high-performing team culture made a lasting impression and has remained a standard for me ever since.

Blur the Lines between All Employees

Improvement cultures often seek to blur the lines between management and people who make products or provide services. Blurring these lines is a significant change from traditional practices that *divide* people between management and workers, white collar and blue collar, or salaried and hourly employees. Making the divisions between managers and nonmanagers obscure is a value linked to broad participation, where all people generate effective solutions to problems and are fully engaged. Management's role is to *support* and *inspire,* not to *direct* and *dictate.*

This change in leadership dynamics requires changes from traditional practices in all aspects of how the organization functions, in order to send a message that truly permeates the culture. I've often asked managers "would you expect to be treated that way for the same situation? Would you expect that if you made a mistake on your daily report, someone would discipline you in writing?" They often say "no;" they would expect to be treated like someone who knows he or she made a mistake and would not require a written notice. I then ask, "Do you think the people you write up for mistakes expect to be given the benefit of the doubt as well about learning from their mistakes?" This issue of blurring the lines between management and nonmanagement is embedded into how people see the world and surely needs to be challenged if you are going to optimize people's talents in the workplace.

Encourage Accountability Instead of Control

Traditional approaches to policies are based on the idea that management needs to create policies that enforce *rules* that prevent people from hurting the organization. In contrast, continuous improvement cultures are based on the idea that people would provide more value if they were allowed to do more. This dynamic can be compared to moving from policies that are based on an "adult–child" relationship to policies that are created with assumptions of "adult–adult" relationships in the workplace. Some say that people live up to the level of expectations; therefore, if an organization treats its people like children, they will behave like children. Equally true, if a company treats its people like adults or as the equals of any member of management, then its people will act like adults. Table 9.2 gives some examples of how behavior differs between adult–child relationships and adult–adult relationships.

Similar to the discussion on how policies may need to be revamped to better align with Lean values, I've seen organizations work to shift policies to a more adult–adult dynamic. The first organization I observed that made significant changes to its policies (to create a culture of mutual respect and

Table 9.2 Review the Tone of Your Organization's Current Policies

Policy	Adult–Adult	Parent–Child
Attendance	People are accountable to their teammates.	People will take advantage of taking days off if you let them.
	Behaviors that are against team goals will be managed by the team.	Policy must stop or monitor people.
Tardiness	People are accountable to each other for getting to work on time.	People will be late if you let them.
	The team needs to decide what level of timeliness is required to accomplish goals.	Policy is needed prevent people from being late or punish them for being late.
Discipline	People are accountable to their teammates.	People will take advantage.
	Behaviors that are against team goals will be managed by the team.	Policy must stop or monitor people.

equality) clearly recognized the link between how employees were counseled and how they would participate in problem solving and process management. I've worked on this issue with several management teams and have met with resistance from some managers who struggle to consider new ideas for managing people beyond the concept that people require control to be productive. Over time, I've found working this topic through a little at a time helps raise awareness until there is broad enough support to truly change how the people are treated.

Communicating Policies via Other Avenues

Communicating Policies via Newsletters, Bulletin Boards, and Meetings

There is a range of communication vehicles by which you can deliver key messages throughout your organization. Furthermore, you can easily integrate continuous improvement messages based on Lean principles into any of these formats, as shown in the chart in Figure 9.1.

From a business partnering perspective, HR can work with any established set of priorities to ensure that a newsletter reflects those objectives.

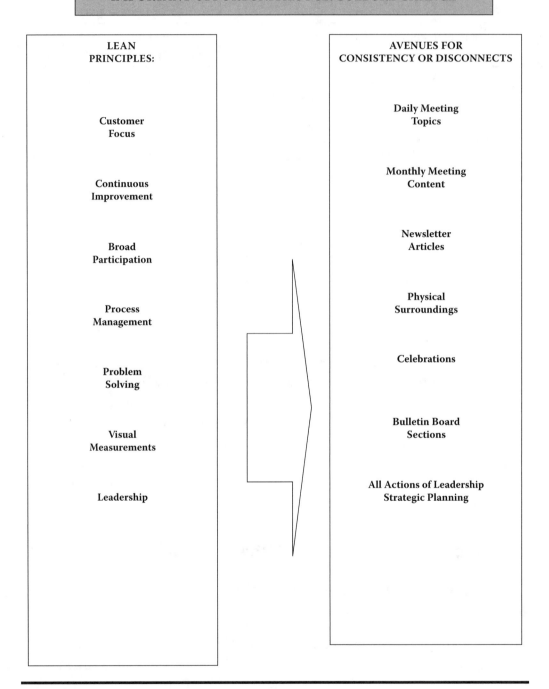

IMPORTANT OPPORTUNITIES FOR CULTURE CHANGE

LEAN
PRINCIPLES:

Customer
Focus

Continuous
Improvement

Broad
Participation

Process
Management

Problem
Solving

Visual
Measurements

Leadership

AVENUES FOR
CONSISTENCY OR DISCONNECTS

Daily Meeting
Topics

Monthly Meeting
Content

Newsletter
Articles

Physical
Surroundings

Celebrations

Bulletin Board
Sections

All Actions of Leadership
Strategic Planning

Figure 9.1   Important opportunities for culture change.

Unfortunately, newsletters, bulletin boards, and repeated meeting formats contain either conflicting messages or are missing opportunities to support culture efforts. I've used newsletters as an effective vehicle for delivering key messages that support cultural initiatives. Each month, every page provides an opportunity to highlight ideas to build the story that needs to be told.

For instance, use your newsletter as a place to communicate team efforts on problem solving. The articles can show the results, the pictures of the teams (which reflects how they work together to get the job done), and the teams smiling as they receive awards for their efforts (which reflects these are behaviors to be repeated for positive recognition). You can have these newsletters reviewed in employee meetings to strengthen their use as a communication vehicle.

Communicating Policy at Celebrations

Next, think about your organization's celebrations and other events and the messages they send. For example, if your organization celebrates only employee birthdays or gives only length-of-service awards, then the message that you're sending to your employees is that you only value the *passage of time*. What does your organization celebrate? If your organization wants to change those messages, how can your celebrations adjust to support this process?

If your organization wants to educate your workforce on how to better run your business, then it is more effective for you to celebrate *business accomplishments*—that is, true improvements, not just yearly milestones—for both and teams. Each of the Lean culture elements reviewed provides an enormous opportunity in the area of celebrations to reinforce concepts. HR professionals can make more significant contributions by supporting the celebrations to strengthen important messages, which requires that they fully understand these issues, not simply order the cake or gifts.

Communicating Culture via Your Organization's Physical Surroundings

Physical surroundings are often an opportunity to create an environment for people that truly encourages them to participate and contribute. Based on the principle of participation, employees can become involved with designing the surroundings that support and enhance their productivity. Because the workplace is a group environment, employees need to be mindful of all people's interests, not just those of a few.

Many organizations with strong cultures have a variety of features in their environment that come from employee participation and concerns. For example, I have toured a facility that makes car parts that had plants growing throughout the middle of the facility under gentle lights to create a more engaging environment. This same facility had a multitude of employees ready to be tour guides to explain why their plant was so attractive and helped them enjoy their day more.

So why does this matter? These same employees could also recount a range of problems they had solved together in teams and the progress they had made on each of their key metrics each month over several years. This was not a facility with a few key talented managers, but a group of highly engaged employees who were achieving superior results by having everyone play a part. Having pictures of their families in their workspaces seemed to reinforce the personal nature of their involvement in their work.

Since then, I have come to believe it's a good idea to allow people to personalize their space as a way to make them more engaged, which certainly includes bringing in reminders of their families and hobbies into their workspace. I've also seen a number of organizations display team-identity materials that promote team spirit. These are simple examples of optimizing people's abilities and contributions within their physical workspace.

Communicating Policy via Your Organization's Safety Programs

Safety programs send very distinct messages to employees that affect their behaviors. Where does safety rank in *your* organization's daily priorities? How do your leaders get involved in safety? What happens when there are accidents? Safety programs can be an area in which to practice improvement methods that build skills while also creating better relationships. Lean methods involve observation, tracking data, conducting root cause analysis to ensure problems don't get repeated, and completing action plans to implement changes for the future. Employees are able to put into practice all these methods on accidents, which helps them build the skills, while they are supported in creating a safer environment for themselves. Safety also provides an area for HR managers to build their skills at improvement to gain more competence and leadership in these areas.

Focusing improvement efforts on issues that clearly create gains to the company and are less focused on employees is less effective than working with employee interests first. Resistance to improvement efforts has been linked to fears or concerns that employees will be hurt if they learn how to remove waste from the environment. I've seen companies do well to focus on safety as a clear opportunity to work with employees to make their lives more comfortable, healthy, and enjoyable, which happens to have benefits for the company as well. As employees gain skills for improvement, those skills can also be applied to other areas of the business that will benefit them, even though at first safety is more apparently about their well being when people are learning these concepts.

Planning Cultural Objectives as Part of Your Strategic Planning

One final area to touch on is aligning your organization's overall planning process to its strategic and cultural objectives. Many organizations have annual planning processes, as well as five-year plans. Cultural planning lends itself to the same types of planning and needs to be linked to these activities.

Similar to the topics just discussed, planning is an area of risk for disconnects with cultural elements. Improvement efforts often involve changes to how customers are serviced, people are engaged, processes are managed, problems are solved, and people are led. The planning processes for each year's activities and goals need to reflect these changes over time.

Also, look for ways strategic plans may actually reflect a lack of alignment with improvement goals or plans that could actually work against your efforts. Although this might seem to be obvious, I've often seen it link to different parts of an organization, or individuals, working on different assignments with little awareness of how they could be better aligned or how they might be working against each other.

Ensure all improvement efforts are integrated into any planning process, as well as that their effects are in alignment with each year's HR strategy, and plan to allow the best results to evolve over time.

In the next chapter, we'll look at how changing a culture can be measured. Part of knowing whether you are achieving your cultural objectives is making sure to measure them. Chapter 10 shows how measuring your culture may be a challenge, but it does provide an avenue to open communication lines around the topics that matter to your organization.

CHAPTER 9 SUMMARY

KEY IDEAS

- Continuous improvement cultures can be seriously damaged or restrained by policies that contradict key messages given in using Lean tools and Lean training.
- HR professionals need to review each policy to evaluate how it aligns with the continuous improvement culture.
- Continuous improvement cultures are generally "adult–adult" work environments, where policies are designed for team accountability.
- Communications in all forms, including newsletters, bulletin boards, and regular meeting topics, can support or damage cultural objectives.
- An organization's physical surroundings should not be overlooked for how they affect people's behavior.
- Strategic planning efforts need to encompass cultural objectives and planning along with other general business plans.

STRATEGIC QUESTIONS FOR HR

1. How would employees behave if policies were not in place to control their behavior? For example, would people still come to work on time if there wasn't a policy in place to control their behavior? How would you need to treat people differently if you wanted them to be responsible for coming to work on time? How could other types of practices, apart from policies, be applied to support the success of the organization and the people within it? _____

_____

_____

_____

_____

_____

_____

_____

_____

2. How could you utilize teams of people, or a participative approach, to re-create policies that need to be revamped to support your cultural objectives? _____

_____

_____

_____

_____

_____

_____

LEAN HR IMPLEMENTATION ACTIONS

1. Audit your organization's policy handbook to identify the types of messages you're sending to employees via your key policies—such as attendance, tardiness, and discipline.

2. Develop a full evaluation and potentially an action plan based on how your organization sees the links and disconnects to desired behaviors and current policies, communications, and practices.

   ■ Meet with senior managers and get their view of what culture would help support the strategic goals. During that conversation, review some of the key policies just mentioned and see how they link with or are disconnected from key cultural objectives.

   ■ Meet with mid-level managers and review their awareness of how key policies might impact cultural objectives that have been communicated already. See if those managers have concerns about how the areas of discipline and attendance affect people's engagement in the workplace.

   – Meet with a sampling of entry-level supervisors and discuss their views of how people respond to discipline and attendance policy. Ask for examples of when someone last made a mistake and how it was handled in terms of any discipline. What kinds of mistakes turn into disciplinary issues and which ones don't? Does it seem consistent among different supervisors? Inquire whether supervisors

believe that people in nonmanagement roles should be
treated differently from people in management and why.
 – Meet with a sampling of employees and get their views of
how these policies impact their engagement.
 – Report findings on the links and disconnects to your proposed culture and consider if changes would strengthen
your culture and hence your results. Be prepared for considerable resistance in this area and to be the change agent
who works to surface these issues. It's not a battle, but a
matter of raising awareness over time. Look for people
who see the issue more clearly, and find ways their support can help turn the tide.

Chapter 10

Can Attitudes Be Measured?

One of the largest challenges in dealing with a culture change of any kind is measuring progress. And many of the changes that are the goal of continuous improvement are particularly difficult to measure because they represent newly acquired viewpoints.

Fortunately, surveys can help; they are an important tool for monitoring changes in employees' attitudes and progress towards cultural objectives. You can conduct a Lean culture survey to measure your employees' attitudes about:

- How they relate to internal and external customers
- Their role in improvement efforts
- Their participation in the workplace
- Processes that support the flow of work
- Solving problems with facts and as a team
- Their understanding of visual goals
- The inspiration (or lack thereof) provided by their leadership

In addition to using surveys to help your organization measure the implementation of a Lean culture (or, in fact, any culture change), you can use surveys to measure your employees' attitudes on any topic that understanding their viewpoint would be helpful in achieving particular goals.

Surveys can measure the success of HR programs and initiatives, where it may be difficult to demonstrate success with any other means or measurements. For example, suppose your organization implemented a new supervisory training program. How could you measure the success of that program? Surveys allow HR to measure how managers treat employees (from the employee's point of view), which provides at least some method to assess whether employees are experiencing a change in their supervisor's abilities or how they are treated by supervisors.

This chapter shows you how to use cultural surveys for any type of culture change, how to use employee-opinion surveys to measure attitudes, and how to use customer surveys to measure customer attitudes. In addition, the chapter discusses the survey process itself to ensure the effort is rewarding for your employees, your customer, and your overall organization. This chapter also addresses one of the biggest concerns about employee surveys, which is that people may often experience a sense of providing their feedback and then not knowing what happens next—so it can create disillusionment that no one cares about their feedback. The process outlined in this chapter includes a number of steps that involve keeping employees informed all along the way about how their feedback is being used to create change.

Surveys Measure Attitudes and Build Relationships

The purpose of a survey is to measure attitudes, but it is also used as a form of communication with employees, which supports relationship building among managers and their teams. The ratings provide an indication of current attitudes as a method to compare to future ratings which records any changes in attitudes. Although surveys are not an exact science, the process is well worth the effort to monitor changes in positions, along with the other information generated by the survey process. In addition to the usefulness of the ratings that measure attitudes, the survey process includes several levels of listening that we'll cover here as well.

Listening Builds Relationships

You can use the ratings and comments on the survey forms to provide a basis for additional conversations with employees. This may be done in small group meetings (as described at the end of this chapter) to learn more about why the ratings are at indicated levels and to co-create actionable next steps from the conversations. Because the ratings themselves are only a numerical sense of employees' responses, or the first level of listening, you need to work on the next level of listening through actual conversations, which together can provide much insight. Comments lack real context unless you explore them for meaning through conversations, which, in turn, provide examples and reveal what respondents would like to see changed.

The process I describe later in the chapter includes steps that allow for follow-up employee meetings with 10% or more of a particular group, to discuss the results and listen in more depth to issues people want to talk about. Employees focus more on wanting to see the actionable next steps that are taken because of their feedback, and those action steps must be communicated for them to be motivated to keep providing feedback.

Many managers may need to build more effective listening skills in the follow-up feedback sessions to help them learn more about how people in their facilities feel about their workplace. For example, I often find that managers are not comfortable having employees make suggestions, and that they often want to *immediately* respond as to why those suggestions "won't work." Yet if you ask someone for feedback and then, at the first suggestion, you tell that person why his or suggestion is wrong, that person will stop giving you the feedback. Many managers need coaching to learn how to ask more questions and be open minded in evaluating ideas *before* responding. Many managers also often defend decisions, rather than listen to why employees may be questioning a decision that has been made. The follow-up meetings allow managers to build relationships by using the written feedback as the start of a communication loop where employees share thoughts, ideas, and concerns, and management really listens to them.

As mentioned, surveys need to be considered as a "listening" process with deeper and deeper levels of listening. The most surface level is the initial ratings, which provide the beginning of important information that needs to be pursued. The comments provide more information, but again, follow-up meetings provide the next level of listening to build understanding. At times, I have found some issues that have been raised through surveys to require many levels of listening, including multiple group meetings that could include everyone in a facility as a group, everyone on an individual basis, or small group meetings, until the topic has been fully explored. Early levels of listening focus on the issues and build into solutions over time. The later meetings may focus on getting feedback on solutions to see if the employees feel those solutions would work.

One topic that may take a wide range of listening exercises is when employees raise significant concerns about being treated fairly or in a non-discriminatory matter. Whatever we might guess their feedback to mean, that is rarely accurate measured against what we uncover through conversations. As employees see considerable effort go to understanding what doesn't seem fair and what might need to be changed, I have attitudes change from fairly dissatisfied to pleased with their work environment.

But as with most efforts, you will only get out of a survey process what you put into it. If you diligently work to understand employee attitudes and to seek positive changes for a more productive and motivated workforce, then the rewards can be many. Basically, your communications should continue until there is a sense that the listening is deep enough to establish important information for guiding future efforts. So although a common complaint of surveys is that the results are not helpful, like all activities that are worthwhile, surveys and listening require patience, perseverance, and strategy to bring greater success.

Let's take a closer look at the three types of surveys most often used, beginning with those regarding culture change.

Using Culture Surveys to Support Culture Changes in Your Organization

The first type of survey is referred to as a *culture survey*, which is used to assess the current attitudes and behaviors of employees. As a tool for improvement, culture surveys begin by evaluating the current condition and can provide information about future targets as well. Measuring progress with culture change efforts is essential for organizations that have invested significant resources in a transformation.

I have commonly seen organizations use tools available in the market place to conduct culture surveys. The Denison Culture Survey is an example of one tool I've seen used to develop a comprehensive understanding of a current culture which laid the foundation for cultural objectives moving forward. A comprehensive survey will ask a wide range of questions and sort the data against each group of employees to provide a picture of how the groups differ in their viewpoints. For managers, this is often the first time they have been able to see in detail how people feel in various departments in a range of roles and what behaviors they think are normal or common in their work environment.

Some organizations may prefer not to use an extensive survey tool to establish touch points to measure their culture and would rather create their own survey.

Construct your culture survey around each of your organization's cultural elements, so you can gauge the current evaluation of the strength of the element and where employees experience disconnects. This tool provides invaluable information about how the concepts are really present in the environment.

For example, suppose you have a culture that contained the elements of innovation, an attitude of customer service, premium products and service, and the golden rule in the workplace. You could create 10–20 questions that explore each of these topics to develop an initial baseline of employee attitudes and then measure whether your efforts to change the culture are successful.

As your organization makes progress and strengthens the desired behavior (or value) in the workplace, the survey monitors the attitudes in some type of objective manner. Then, your follow-up activities can also provide significant opportunities to further understand how the value or concept is being understood by the workers. For culture change to be meaningful, it is important to direct efforts to understand what people are experiencing and not just allow wishful thinking to prevail.

Taking Surveys of Employee Satisfaction

Employee surveys are another type of survey; in general, these can be used separately from culture surveys because they should focus more on employee concerns. Satisfaction surveys would then measure employee morale levels overall and canvas for particular issues related to satisfaction and dissatisfaction so you can find areas of opportunity for change. The survey gives an initial baseline, but changes in results provide some indication that efforts towards boosting employee morale are resulting in increased satisfaction.

For example, if your company has conducted a series of training activities to build the supervisory skills for entry-level supervisors, how would you know if the training is having an effect on employee morale? I have generally seen that areas of an organization that need improved supervisory skills show low ratings on how people feel they are treated. When those skills are improved through training and ongoing coaching, the ratings will go up. If they don't, it's time to examine whether the right people are supervising the area or if the training/coaching intervention is effective. Surveys allow for a communication process to find out what is real to employees and what is not.

Surveys also help HR, as a business partner, validate various types of HR interventions and programs in terms of increased satisfaction levels. An underlying assumption of employee surveys is that happier or more satisfied employees are more productive, have less turnover, and are more engaged in their work.

Common topics for employee surveys regarding HR programs are on-boarding, training, career planning, benefits, pay fairness, and recognition. Employee surveys also cover working conditions such as facilities, hours, or uniforms. Table 10.1 provides a list of some of the areas you might ask your employees to comment on.

Table 10.1 Sample List of Survey Topics for Employees

Survey Questions	Ratings 1–10
1. I am clear about how my work links to customers.	
2. I understand the needs of our customers as they relate to my work.	
3. I would like to better understand the needs of our customers.	
4. I see that we regularly make gains in my area.	
5. I know how to use tools to improve our results.	
6. I know what I can control to improve the results in my area.	
7. I would like to know more about how to improve my area of the business.	
8. I understand the whole process that I work on each day.	
9. I understand parts of the process that are not in my area.	
10. I would like to learn more about process management.	
11. I am able to participate in management decisions that affect me.	
12. I feel my ideas for resolving challenges in my area are regularly sought.	
13. I would like to participate more on a daily basis.	
14. I have been trained and understand how to solve problems with facts.	
15. I would like to be more educated and practiced in problem solving.	
16. We have visible metrics in my area.	
17. I understand the visible metrics in my area.	
18. I would like to better understand the metrics in my area.	
19. I find my manager to be of great support to my area.	
20. I believe my manager sees his or her role as being to support my growth.	
21. I would like more support from my manager.	

Note: Rating, 1–10, where 1 = "strongly disagree" and 10 = "strongly agree."

Customer Surveys Can Be Very Useful

In alignment with the value on customers, *customer satisfaction surveys* are another helpful tool for improvement. Customer surveys enable you to measure customer satisfaction, and they provide a mechanism to gather information about your customers' concerns, interests, problems, and needs.

The purpose of customer surveys may be to support strategic planning, marketing efforts, or customer service improvements. They can also address specific concerns or simply be proactive in helping your organization understand your customers' concerns and interest.

I first implemented the use of a customer survey to better understand our current levels of service. We created a list of five questions, and we then had a small group of people call our larger customers and review their answers. The focus of the phone calls was learning how customers perceived the current level of customer service, and what areas of our service failed to meet their expectations. We gathered ideas on where our customers wanted to see improvement.

I recall that the customers raised a number of concerns about how billing was handled, in terms of accurate pricing and how discounts were reflected. Based on this survey process, several billing changes were made that were given high marks from our customers for better meeting their needs.

This customer survey was an example not only of how the billing improvements could make a difference, but how asking our customers the question about what would make their life easier created an opportunity to strengthen our relationship and better meet their needs. This survey process was part of a process improvement team's efforts to improve the order fulfillment process and was part of that group's learning how to use customer input to guide improvement efforts.

The format for customer surveys varies and may include multiple formats to gather in-depth information to improve services, identify new needs with revenue potential, and clarify how the customer's needs are currently being met. The surveys may be done by in-person interviews, phone interviews, or written survey responses, among others. Interviews allow you to collect more detailed information.

In the example just discussed, we used a few questions to have a conversation with our customers. We were careful to have someone call the customer who was not part of that customer's current service staff, so the customer would feel free to provide honest feedback. The types of issues we sorted through included how to get to the right person within the customer's organization, under what conditions would they provide honest feedback, and what methods would positively affect our relationship with them.

For instance, we decided that sending out a written survey to canvas feedback would likely not work well with our customers, and they might find it irritating. We found that calling them with specific questions they could address and provide feedback to better meet their needs was mostly enjoyable for our customers and hence a good design. Generally speaking, a customer who is key to your organization wants to strengthen the communication to improve the links between your organizations. HR can use the skills from employee surveys to teach others in the organization how surveys can be a tremendous tool in better understanding needs.

The level of resources and amount of attention given to customer surveys vary, on the needs and insights obtained.

Similar to employee surveys, customer surveys are a listening tool that requires more than analyzing ratings to fully understand the feedback. Also similar to employee surveys, HR professionals can use their survey and communication skills to partner with the sales force, to conduct customer surveys to enhance services, and improve customer satisfaction. The elements of increasing employee satisfaction as *internal* customers are the same as those needed for increasing *external* customer satisfaction.

The Survey Process

Some organizations may not currently have survey processes. Organizations that do have survey processes may be disappointed with their results, as they are often managed in a way that fails to achieve substantial results. The disappointment is often from the fact the survey results are not used for anything beneficial, and the ratings themselves fail to provide much useful information. It stands to reason that if people see that time spent providing suggestions and ideas is used to better their work life, then they will enthusiastically participate. However, management will need to be diligent about ensuring that people are not wasting their time in providing the feedback, either because next steps aren't taken or the actions aren't communicated to people in a way that sufficiently reflects attentiveness to their feedback.

When I've seen managers struggle with the follow-up portion of the survey process, it generally reflects their attitudes about their relationships with their team members. Lack of attention may not mean they have a bad attitude about people, but it can mean that they aren't thinking of the need to tend to their relationships with people as a part of a healthy workplace.

Surveys often fail to make use of the data in a manner participants appreciate. The following process is designed to show you how to fully listen to the issues and ideas of the participants, while keeping the larger group fully informed as to what is transpiring in the communication process. However, before even implementing the steps below, it's important to keep in mind that the burning question for survey participants is "What will be done with my feedback that makes this worth my time?"

- Step 1: Develop survey questions that meet the objectives in the process. Ensure clear objectives are identified in creating the questions. Do not collect needless data.
- Step 2: Conduct surveys with a goal of at least 50% participation. Surveys can be administered during employee meals or celebrations to increase participation.
- Step 3: Communicate results to all participants to make them aware of overall feedback and that further evaluation is being performed to create responses and actions.
- Step 4: Make sure the leadership team constructs follow-up questions based on the results and survey comments.
- Step 5: The written comments and ratings on the questions are only the beginning of this listening process. Hold small focus group discussions with approximately 10% of employees who took the survey to talk about the survey results and gain more insights about employee concerns and, more important, to hear their ideas about what could be changed to improve their ratings.
- Step 6: Based on your conversations with employees, gather their ideas about possible actions that could be taken to improve their situation in the workplace. The action items need to be put into some type of written format so they can be tracked over time.
- Step 7: Communicate action plans to all participants and other interested parties. The action plans need to be simple and include timelines for employees to track the program against them.
- Step 8: Communicate progress with action plans to participants and other parties.

■ Step 9: The survey process needs to be repeated with some frequency to monitor changes in ratings, as well as to continue the conversations with employees about concerns in the workplace.

For many organizations, the survey process is one of the only two-way communication vehicles they have in their workplace. I have often found that managers don't see the survey tool as important because getting the current workload done hasn't required them to better understand employee viewpoints. I cannot emphasize enough that optimizing people's abilities in the workplace requires a range of two-way communication options; surveys are a good foundation for measuring your progress with communications. The next section of this book will detail how various HR programs (i.e., job content, recruiting, training, performance management, and rewards) need to be redesigned to allow your employees to contribute so much more. The survey process also provides a method to measure how well the changes to HR programs are working based on an employee viewpoint, which, after all, is the voice of the customer inside your workplace.

CHAPTER 10 SUMMARY

KEY IDEAS

■ Surveys are an important tool to measure culture changes.
■ Culture change can be measured by surveys designed to evaluate employees' current attitudes and values to assess if your organization's initiatives to change your culture are effective.
■ Employee satisfaction surveys also support change by reinforcing the relationships in the workplace that need to drive results.
■ Customer surveys are another feature of continuous improvement cultures, which are heavily customer focused.

STRATEGIC QUESTIONS FOR HR

1. How do you currently measure your overall culture? _____

_____

_____

_____

_____

2. How consistently do your employees experience important messages or values in your environment? Would surveys help you
   better understand what your employees experience? _____

_____

_____

_____

_____

LEAN HR IMPLEMENTATION ACTIONS

1. Based on your organization's key cultural elements, create and
   conduct a culture survey to determine your organization's current alignment to your desired culture.

   - Map the results of the survey to type of job roles and to
     areas of your processes, to see where there are differences
     in alignment and to identify areas that potentially need to
     be given priority.

   - After a baseline is established, you can repeat the culture
     survey to measure whether your efforts at culture changes are
     having the desired effect.

   - The written survey process is only one aspect of this listening
     process. Be sure to follow up with people to discuss results
     and co-create actionable plans to make improvements to
     enhance cultural alignment.

2. Conduct employee satisfaction or engagement surveys to gauge
   current employee morale and create two-way dialogs about
   issues of concern to employees.

   - Be sure to use this process as a way to enhance leadership's
     relationship with employees and not just make it a simple
     measurement of current satisfaction levels.

   - Keep in mind that making changes in response to employee
     feedback that improves the quality of life for the workforce is
     an important primer to seeking employee participation that
     will also improve workplace functioning. Employees learn
     participation better when it applies to their benefit first.

3. Conduct a customer survey to gain insights into your customers' concerns and values that will improve your organization's value to your customers over time.

- A customer survey can be part of an improvement team's work to ensure internal changes are made with the customer in mind.
- Ensure strong communication skills are applied to fully listen to customer feedback, and get back to customers who participate with information on what changes have been made in response to their feedback.

REDESIGN ROLES FOR BETTER RESULTS

The last section provides a framework for identifying the culture you want to create in a manner that drives your strategic results. As HR plays an even larger role in implementing the needed behaviors and attitudes in the workplace for the desired results, the jobs and HR processes must also be redesigned.

Therefore, this section is devoted to creating a framework for how to put behaviors and attitudes into job content which can then be the basis for all other HR programs that link to job performance. Chapter 11 starts with how the job content needs to be overhauled reflect a culture of continuous improvement. Chapter 12 gives a detailed approach on how to create the documentation that supports the change in job content but also provides a framework for all HR programs.

Chapter 11

Optimize Each Job

Based on how your business strategy aligns with your desired culture and values, this chapter details how you can build behaviors into actual jobs or specific roles. Because continuous improvement or Lean strategies heavily emphasize the contribution of all people, the task of building Lean principles into each job is imperative to successful results. The principles break down into critical behaviors, results, and underlying abilities that deliver superior performance. The end of this chapter offers a brief summary of how to customize these job requirements. The process of building strategy and culture into each job is done through a competency model, which is then the basis for most HR programs as it establishes a common set of skills or abilities (which is covered in Chapter 12).

Building Continuous Improvement into Jobs

All jobs involve competencies, which are the skills or abilities required within each particular job. A competency model includes four types of competency groupings for job content:

1. **Organization wide**—this refers to the skills or abilities needed from the majority of people within the organization. These would be prevalent in common work and something to strive for with all employees.
2. **Anyone in a leadership or management role**—leadership competencies create a standard for managers in terms of their leadership roles. Most of the organizational competencies require managers to support those skills by managing in a manner that supports those behaviors.

3. **By function**—these competencies would be different for various functions, such as operations, accounting, human resources, quality assurance, and information systems. The functional competencies link to the organizational competencies, but they have different standards required for the skills or specific applications that are relevant only to that department.

4. **By position for job-specific detail**—these competencies will also be linked to the other competencies, but they will be set at a level appropriate for the precise job and may be tailored to particular needs.

A continuous improvement competency model takes this traditional competency approach and ensures the needs of a continuous improvement culture with the desired results being threaded into all jobs. This ensures that the desire to create a particular environment goes into a specific type of plan to build these skills into the jobs on a long-term basis. Although changing job content can take a significant amount of time, the results will also be relatively long lasting.

The model begins with the organizational competencies (Level 1), which are those that are required for all jobs. The competencies would then be universal across the organization. This chapter presents specific continuous improvement competencies, but you can customize them to fit the particular needs of your organization. The Lean HR Competency Model as shown in Figure 11.1 takes a traditional competency approach and ensures each aspect of a continuous improvement culture is threaded into each and every job. The Lean HR Competency Model, or a customized model of your choice, creates your intended workplace based upon a plan that builds the needed skills and required behaviors into the jobs on a long-term basis. Establishing the Level 1 competencies for your organization will be the largest part of your Lean HR implementation, but it is often not the place organizations will begin to put Lean requirements into job content. Also, to be clear, Level 1 does not refer to working on all non-managerial roles, but usually begins with a few key roles that are held by relatively large groups of people to implement cultural objectives. More often, organizations begin with establishing Lean leadership competencies in Level 2. Department specific competencies are built into jobs as needed changes are identified that support that department in adding more value in terms of meeting customer needs and optimizing their processes. Upon completion of your model, there will be a design for the gold standards of each and every job role, the Level 4 job competencies. Some competencies might be picked up in Level 4 that are specific to only one job and this is where those details are registered.

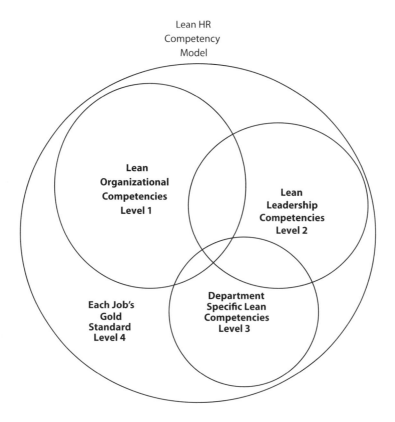

Figure 11.1   Lean HR competency model.

For example, I recently visited an organization that wanted everyone to be involved in having the skills to providing and implementing employee suggestions for improvement, which is an example of a Level 1 competency. The managers, or Lean leaders, were required to supervise the suggestion process, which included implementing ideas and coaching others to support the implementation of ideas, which is a Level 2 competency. The HR depart-ment had to build skills in the area of training managers and employees in their roles of the suggestion process, which would be a Level 3 competency. Lastly, there was one person who had the specific role to communicate for all stakeholders the full range of employee suggestions and their implemen-tations in a manner that drove increasing amounts of them, which would be a Level 4 job specific competency. Understanding the competencies described here in Chapter 11 will become the basis for documenting these requirements as shown in Chapter 12. Chapter 12 shows how you can then document these job requirements.

Level 1: Everyone Actively Drives Continuous Improvement

All Roads Lead to the Customer

Many organizations, including those that are continuous improvement oriented, have a strategy and culture that includes a focus on the customer.
However, to ensure that customer focus is part of the job requirements,
the competencies or skills should reflect this focus in terms of *specific*
skills or behaviors. Customer-related skills would include maintaining customer awareness as the basis of work activities as well as ensuring general
customer service principles are broadly applied. These skills can benefit
a business by having employees ensure their work is focused on the customer, which helps eliminate problems and helps handle them well when
they arise. More important, providing customer focus in the workplace gives
meaning to the work of employees, who work better with a sense of purpose, instead of just focusing on the tasks at hand.

The skills for maintaining awareness of customer's needs generally
involve a range of activities to inform employees about customers and as the
basis for most important decisions. HR can have an important role in supporting this communication challenge.

For example, working closely with the sales department, I have seen HR
create communication materials that highlight information about customers
and their needs. Customer information can be put into daily employee briefings, bulletin board postings, larger employee meetings, and any communication vehicle that has room to include customer information. Over time,
I have noticed that employees are more enthusiastic about making activity-
supporting work processes, once they have grown to better understand their
customers' needs.

For instance, there was a time that our largest customer had complained
about damaged boxes arriving in its warehouse. We kept educating our
employees about this issue, with pictures and details of the customer concern in our daily meetings and weekly improvement sessions. Over time, we
made several changes in how boxes were packed and loaded into trucks.
The employees were at the front of the changes as they realized the risk this
issue placed to their jobs, as well as the benefit of resolving the problem.

Our customer was happy that we not only fixed the problem but that it
was our warehouse employees who designed the fix and communicated their
new process to them. It let the customer know that the people who work on
their goods are the ones who care enough to figure out better methods. It also

let our employees know that they were capable of understanding a business problem, resolving it, and then communicating their work to upper management and the customer (which was a real boost to their self esteem!).

HR may also participate in developing training materials that teach customer service skills as well as specific customer requirements. I have provided training in customer service skills for broader groups of employees in the following areas:

- How to surface customer needs;
- how to generate possible solutions to customer needs; and
- how to handle disgruntled customers effectively.

Lean values and competencies are similar in terms of topics, but the competencies convert the underlying assumptions into specific job requirements that involve accountability for specific behaviors. Putting the desired culture and related behaviors into the required job contents is a major change that produces significant results, but has often not been part of efforts to more fully utilize people and improve results.

For example, our HR department was told the accounting department was having a range of problems with the way payroll was being submitted. By teaching our team of HR professionals to surface needs of customers (anyone you feed information to is a "customer" of your work or process), they knew how to surface the problem with another department, and then call a meeting to identify concerns and develop action plans to resolve deficiencies. Customers prefer to work with organizations that involve active learning to prevent future mistakes, which is part of the next competency.

Everyone Needs to Learn and Improve

A core element of continuous improvement cultures is improved results over time. This absolutely requires an extensive ability to learn. As a required competency across an organization, it is a general requirement that people seek improvement and participate in improvement activities—which is a form of learning. This makes it clear that jobs are not just a matter of maintaining a set of tasks, but adjusting those tasks over time to have ever improving results. I have found that it is important this be stated as a *requirement,* not a suggestion, to support the momentum needed in change efforts and to reduce resistance to new ways of doing things. The more the standard is to learn and change for better results, the more people have that as a "frame of reference."

HR has an important role in helping management create an environment that requires improvement as a part of jobs. While HR can help provide training on methods of improvement, they also need to work with managers to integrate those methods into daily job tasks so they become part of daily work.

For example, if employees are trained in learning about waste, including measuring progress and observing work to identify new ideas for improvement, that type of skill and work task needs to be built into their jobs *as part of their work,* instead of simply being a training module that has long been forgotten or was only to be used that particular day or week. As HR builds improvement and learning into jobs, it is closely linked with communication, which is the next competency.

Everyone Needs to Participate and Be Involved

As people learn, they need to be able to communicate effectively with one another. Because participation and involvement are cornerstones of Lean companies, it requires heightened communication skills. Building participation, involvement, and communication competencies into jobs can be done in a number of ways. Communications can involve participation in daily meetings, as well as specific process requirements.

For example, a process might require that problems be communicated through a log and that the person follow up to ensure the problem is being addressed. I have seen the majority of process teams include communication systems or methods to ensure critical information is passed along when needed. Therefore, highlighting communication skills and requirements into job content is part of making sure this expectation is clearly communicated itself.

Involvement may be developed as a competency that requires suggestions to be made as a part of regular work. Employees may be required to provide two suggestions per year, or one per month, as a part of the work. Although these suggestions may be rewarded, it's important that any activity that is meant to be part of the daily work be seen as such.

Participation may include requirements to work on specific teams to improve results and solve problems. Although there may be some requirements of this in the jobs, work can be designed so that people in all levels of jobs are able to participate effectively in problem solving and other inter-departmental teams.

The role of HR in maintaining (if not developing) an environment in which people feel safe and respected enough to share their ideas depends on the awareness that this is essential for obtaining the participation for improved results. For example, I developed a course called "Sharing Your Ideas" that mostly focused on how people needed to treat each other when they took the risk of bringing their ideas into the workplace. Every employee participated in the brief course, and over time, we noticed a growing comfort with the idea that sharing ideas was considered "sacred" or "valuable" so it needed to be treated with care and importance. Communicating effectively will then support more detailed work related to process management.

Everyone Knows the Business to Some Degree

Organization-wide process management skills involve having a broad group of employees (if not all of them) participate in improvement activities by developing and executing actionable plans that improve the results of a particular process. Process management activities are best supported by providing a broad amount of business knowledge and process management training to build the necessary skills in these areas. I have also seen requirements for people to be productive members of teams beyond their traditional work groups as a job requirement as well.

The goal with providing business knowledge is to have all employees learn basic financial information about your business as well as basic elements of your sales and marketing plans. HR can help develop and teach the training materials that provide employees the information about your specific organization's financials and sales plans. I have found training employees about your business is hugely beneficial to employees in improving their work, as they come to a greater understanding of how to make better decisions using fundamental financial information.

Beyond finance-related training, process management skills involve teaching people how they relate to the bigger picture of meeting customer needs in the marketplace. I have facilitated teams in understanding how they work together by sharing their perspectives from different points of the process. These insights invariably create gains in developing improved methods of working, which is also part of process management. In fact, one of the primary goals of ensuring everyone understands all the processes involved in meeting customer needs, instead of just the piece they are contributing to, is that it greatly enhances problem-solving capabilities as will be reviewed next.

Everyone Participates in Team Problem Solving

To develop an approach of team-based factual problem solving involves a relatively complex set of skills for an organization. Generally, problem solving is an ability present in all people, but it is severely underutilized. Problem-solving skills can certainly be taught, and people have the inherent ability to solve problems.

The issue beyond training is how to develop mechanisms or processes to involve much broader groups of people in problem solving. Generally, this competency is built in stages, and a Lean effort is in mature phases before these skills and abilities are broadly applied to all employees.

The HR group is a critical component to detailing the job content and developing the training materials and supporting the facilitation needs required to resolve problems in teams. I have had more than one HR department develop the actual training materials that are used to teach fact-based problem solving and had HR people conduct the training as well. The training has generally included a series of steps for solving problems; methods for uncovering the root causes; methods to gather data to better understand situations; and ways to implement the solutions to the issues discovered. The material is readily available for HR to customize to your organization and to begin teaching from it.

Organizations that build problem solving into job content often require that employees be able to identify and resolve the root causes of problems, often in a team setting. I have seen problem-solving requirements also include being able to gather information as well as requesting support from management based on data-based solutions. Similar to process management, job content related to problem solving may involve requiring workers to be functional members of teams with the corresponding skills that go into teamwork.

Because problem solving is often done in teams, I've also had HR develop team skills that help support problem-solving teams as well. Team skills include team leadership, team facilitation, and roles for team members. Again, HR can support the objectives of other departments by helping supply the training and processes to help groups improve their results. Because fact-based problem solving often requires reference to facts to ensure the problem is well understood, these facts frequently become part of the visual measurements in the workplace.

Everyone Knows Which Measurements Relate to Them

Similar to the business knowledge mentioned above on a broad level, Lean organizations often need most employees to understand the key metrics of their immediate area. Often, people are working with no idea of how well they are doing. Lean environments commonly involve visual measurements that ensure people know how well they are doing. This dynamic can create stresses and pressures that need to be managed to create a positive force rather than a problematic structure.

To help employees work against measurements, HR can provide training and support for goal-setting skills as well as the business knowledge required to improve measurements. As people understand their measurements, new leaders emerge as well. (Level 2 provides more information on how to lead with visual measurements.)

Everyone Can Lead

Leadership in a continuous improvement culture is not an honor saved for the few people "in charge." Instead, personal leadership as a behavior, not a position, is an option available to all employees with a range of opportunities to explore how to display leadership in new ways. Here are just a few examples:

- Leadership could involve anyone who participates on a problem-solving team coming up with an idea that helps improve the workflow and solve a problem.
- Leadership could be sharing an idea at an employee meeting and then volunteering to help implement it going forward.
- Leadership could be role modeling important behaviors that help the business succeed, such as supporting a teammate who needs help.
- Leadership could involve recognizing a customer issue that needs attention and might include solving the issue as well.

Expanding the view of leadership and each individual's ability and need to explore his or her leadership is a hallmark of Lean cultures. I've had the HR department facilitate the weekly departmental meetings where employees are encouraged to share their ideas. A number of leaders will surface in these meetings whose leadership may not have been apparent during their normal work routines.

HR can also develop the materials that inspire employees to explore their own personal leadership in new ways. For instance, I've had HR provide workshops on teamwork that have inspired people who don't appear to see themselves as leaders to step forward and help their own teams (i.e., normal work groups) do better together and achieve higher goals. I've also seen the need for HR to work closely with each department and the managers to ensure they are encouraging people at all levels to be leaders in a variety of ways, as they work on problems and generate ideas for improvement.

Level 2: Winning or Losing Often Links to the Right Leadership

Leadership competencies are part of the job content for individuals in management roles who supervise people. Versions of these competencies would also be in the jobs of front-line supervisors who might be paid on an hourly basis, but who still supervise people. The information in this section states the competencies for a mid-range manager. These same competencies would be set at a level that requires more or less skill, depending on the leadership role. These competencies are based on the visionary and inspirational leadership model that was described in Chapter 7.

In other words, leadership's role in a continuous improvement environment is to inspire people into levels of contribution they may not have ever achieved or experienced. Therefore, the need to lay out new leadership requirements is critical to achieving this vision. Reflecting the fundamental concept of a Lean culture in Figure 11.2, achieving better results from the majority of your people is based upon working with leaders that allow for the optimization of everyone's contributions.

Lead with the Customer in Mind

Leaders in a continuous improvement culture need to model how to put the customer first, which is an application of the first common Lean Principles or cultural elements. Managers who demonstrate this skill explain changes

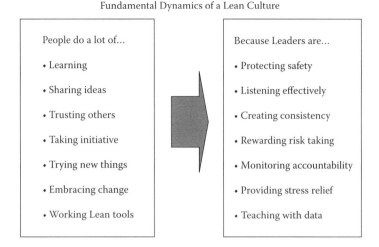

Figure 11.2   **Fundamental dynamics of a Lean culture.**

to their team, when possible, in light of customers' needs. It's been my experience that the more specific a manager is about the customer (e.g., his or her first name, what job he or she has at the customer's company, and why that customer is loyal to your company), the more people focus on getting the job done—and with a sense of urgency as well. Therefore, the management style of these leaders is to regularly demonstrate what it means to put the customer first. For example, a manager would explain work in terms of its impact on customers and always link issues back to how they affect customers as specifically as possible. Managers need to make customers more real to employees by letting them know as much as possible about the people to whom they provide services or products, including what is important to them and any current issues with a particular customer.

Making decisions in light of how they impact customers and their needs is an example of leading by customer orientation. For example, imagine a situation in which a customer group needs to change its approach to quality checks and requires that a completely new report be completed by the person working on a particular production line. To demonstrate customer focus, you would have employee meetings to discuss the situation that had led the customer to require this change, including pictures of the customer's quality controls in its facilities. Linking the new report to the customer with a great amount of detail would lead to a more successful completion of the new report or a new duty, because the customer had become more real.

HR can play a role in documenting this type of competency as part of managers' responsibilities. In addition, HR can support the gathering of information from the sales force to bring in operational areas to support needed changes or alert employees to particular issues that need attention. HR can coach leaders in considering how employees feel or respond to changes if the customer needs are communicated in concrete terms with sufficient detail to truly understand the meaning behind their work. HR needs to support leaders in giving work meaning, so employees work with a greater sense of mission and purpose and are able to embrace change when needed. "Customer first," the first of the common Lean principles, is one way leaders teach, and teaching is the basis of the next competencies of Lean leaders.

Lead by Teaching and Coaching

Continuous improvement, the second common Lean cultural element, becomes pervasive in your workplace when leaders predominantly teach and coach (so that people learn) instead of manage people. The results improve exponentially when leaders or managers are required to be able to coach effectively in the eyes of their mentees and to effectively create an environment where people learn from every aspect of their work. If you want people to learn from historical results, then you need leaders who teach. Teaching is much different than managing in a traditional sense, in that it is a matter of using questions for people to learn from situations rather than just giving them the answers or being punitive about mistakes.

The principle of teaching is broadly applied to managers in a Lean culture and may be referred to as *coaching* to differentiate this style of leadership from behaviors and attitudes associated with managing people. Traditionally, managers are seen as *controlling* people to ensure the right thing happens and to prevent people from doing the wrong things. In contrast, coaching is a *supportive* role that unleashes the skills and talents of people and provides a path for each person to discover his or her potential, which can be squelched under too much control.

Lean organizations obtain markedly different results when their supervisory efforts are structured as "coaching" instead of managing others. For example, I've seen one organization dramatically change its supervisory roles to "coaching roles" and develop much higher levels of skills in the majority of its workforce, as barriers were removed that allowed people to make more decisions, schedule work, deal with customers, and do other tasks generally considered the work of "supervisors."

Apart from the leadership style of coaching, continuous improvement requires extensive learning by applying useful lessons in at least three ways:

1. Demonstrate how to use work methods or the practices of other companies or departments as a way to learn how to develop improved methods (referred to as *span of learning*). For example, you could have a manager show that the way his or her department uses its visible boards in the facility was learned from another division of the company.

2. Demonstrate how to use daily, weekly, or monthly data to make changes to current practices (referred to as *rate of learning*). For example, a manager might use daily data to have his team learn what adjustments need to be made to achieve the desired weekly results, as opposed to waiting a few weeks after month's end to respond to the need for adjustments.

3. Demonstrate how to get at underlying issues or root causes of issues to make changes that will improve results (referred to as *depth of learning*). For example, a manager would keep asking her team members to consider why things are happening, instead of giving them quick answers to what they need to do differently. Teach people to think for themselves and to realize that most situations have several layers of causes that need to be addressed for improved results.

Building these types of teaching methods provides obvious benefits to an organization. Yet strengthening the skills to help people learn faster, more efficiently, and with better understanding to impact results is a challenge that HR has a role in supporting. There could be a requirement that employees participate in sessions to learn better ways of doing things.

Leaders Who Inspire Participation, Listen Effectively, and Reward Initiative

Participation is the third common Lean principle for Lean leaders, and includes a range of skills for leaders, including the ability to listen effectively, to encourage regular participation, and to reward initiative. Leaders in a Lean culture need to *inspire* people to perform; they can't *mandate* people to participate.

Inspiration involves encouraging and supporting people, and helping people think more of themselves. Leaders need to be aware of people's self-esteem needs and work to prevent negative consequences from handling situations poorly. These leaders actively protect their relationships with everyone around them, with the most focus on their team. These leaders also support a culture or environment that has clear lines of acceptable behavior that involves treating people with respect and dignity at all times, which involves listening well if you are going to develop broad participation.

Listening effectively to encourage participation involves creating opportunities for people to share, such as daily briefings, weekly departmental meetings, survey meetings, or written suggestion programs. Listening requires carefully considering people's ideas and suggestions, which includes effective responses that generate more ideas, etc.

HR can play a role by teaching classes in which people experience how they like to feel listened to in terms of the other person's focus, making eye contact, and being open-minded and respectful of each other's ideas. Yet most managers will admit they struggle with paying this level of attention to their team members every day, because of daily stresses and distractions. In addition, most managers agree that one time of failing to really listen to someone is often their last chance before that person stops sharing altogether. Therefore, organizations that want people to share ideas need to ensure that their managers become much more conscious of how they are responding to people and the consequences of treating them in ways that they themselves wouldn't like to be treated.

These classes also teach ways to make suggestions and the responses visible for everyone to encourage others to provide them as well. The other skill that is a critical part of listening effectively to teammates is asking questions. Most managers agree that they tend to want to simply *give the answer*, not ask questions to help uncover more about what a teammate is discussing and to help him or her find an answer to the problem. Creating participation in the workplace takes more time, attention to people's feelings, and higher levels of communication skills than might be found in traditional work settings. HR will have a role to play in developing the training and supporting the ongoing coaching to build these skills into daily life.

Last, rewarding initiative does not necessarily involve financial recognition. It is possible to recognize positive contributions with gift cards, stamps, company logo shirts, pictures in the newsletter, and visits from the president of the company. Every suggestion demands positive recognition, no matter how small the contribution or simple recognition. HR should be involved in developing the recognition processes for supporting these ideas.

Lead with a Standard of Consistency

As a leader, a manager needs to obtain consistent results by applying a sustainable process to any given work set, which supports the fourth common Lean principle, process management. Managing to obtain consistency ensures good results can be repeated and improved on with a scientific method or approach. The Lean leader may need to build skills in process management, process improvement, and working to target to achieve superior financial results. These leaders look at problems as opportunities to improve processes.

Leaders in Lean environments teach customer orientation in part by also considering internal functions to be part of a customer supply chain. For example, a manager in the finance department would lead by considering people who utilize financial statements as "customers" and would therefore make decisions with the needs of those "customers" in mind. When you teach *internal* customer orientation, people quickly see the link between their specific work and your *external* customers.

Managers in Lean environments actually *encourage* surfacing problems, because achieving superior results is founded in identifying and resolving issues so they are not repeated. Problem solving, the fifth common Lean principle, is one of the most important area of skill and required competency of Lean leaders.

Prevent Problems by Encouraging People to Surface Them

HR has a role in supporting this competency in being able to effectively document it as a foundation for recruitment, training, accountability, and rewards. In order for HR departments to be fully involved and support this work in all HR programs, they need to understand a process-driven environment that is committed to consistency, including the managers that effectively work in them. If this area is overlooked or undermanaged, that will undermine the very culture needed for sustainable results over time.

For example, suppose your organization has made a terrible mistake that creates a tremendous upset with a customer. A leader would need to figure out how to teach people by asking them questions about how the mistake happened and what effect they believe it would have on the customer. The leader would also use questions to invite people to explore new ways of working in the future for better results. Leaders might have opportunities to invite some people to work directly with the customer as part of their learning and a way to show the customer that your organization is committed to learning from mistakes (to prevent repeating them).

Being able to convince employees that surfacing problems is encouraged can be a daunting task. Therefore, HR has a significant role in helping the organization understand the psychological safety required for this element of the culture. For example, many employees may be disciplined for mistakes or for their part of a problem, which is distinctly counter to an environment that wants to uncover problems. Many areas that are managed or supported by HR need to be revised to best support a culture that surfaces problems enthusiastically.

Once problems are surfaced, problem solving needs to be factually based. Generally, people will tend to jump to conclusions and often fix issues that are not the cause of identified problems. Therefore, to achieve improved results, it is critical to develop a methodical approach that teaches people to get past their habits of simply guessing and reacting to situations. Again, Lean HR shows a significant role for the HR department to provide the training, facilitation, accountability, and recognition of individuals and teams that use team-based factual problem solving on a regular basis.

Last, working in teams may not always be feasible, but it is a hallmark of continuous improvement cultures. Teamwork is required for more interdisciplinary problems, because many processes cover more than one department. Problem solving will be based on facts that are within identified processes. Therefore, everyone in the process typically is represented in these teams to resolve issues.

Lead with Visual Measurements

Managers in continuous improvement workplaces almost always lead with visual measurements, which is the sixth of the Lean principles. As mentioned in the description of Level 1, employees or associates need to be able to see how they are doing in order to participate in improvement efforts. Lean leaders are well versed in using visual measurements to help people understand key areas of focus and to know on an hour-by-hour basis how they are doing against daily, weekly, and monthly goals. Lean leaders believe visual measurements are critical to achieving their results. Having every single person pulling towards common goals, with timely information on how they are tracking, is a fundamental component of continuous improvement cultures.

HR may be involved in developing the skills to keep measurements simple and easy to see and to use techniques involving color, timeliness, and ways to reflect vital information on the results of an area. HR may also be involved in supporting elements such as recognition and rewards against the attainment of goals, which is a great opportunity for HR to help leaders accomplish their goals.

Lead by Creating More Leaders

The management or leadership competency of creating new leaders is relatively difficult to accomplish as the seventh common Lean principle of inspirational leadership. These leaders do not appear to control things and deflect the appearance they directly handle many matters of importance. These leaders do create conditions for success for others by providing direction, parameters, support for overcoming obstacles, and achievable goals.

In addition, these leaders surface the ideas of others and do not rely only on their own ideas to produce the best results. These leaders understand that motivation is a critical component of obtaining results through people, so they develop leaders who are able to motivate others. The techniques of these leaders empower others to grow and become less dependent on receiving direction from others. In general, these individuals are knowledgeable about the philosophy of Lean and are able to demonstrate the ability to develop leaders in these principles.

HR may be involved in providing a range of skill-development support to train leaders be able to develop others. This may include coursework on methods for managing people differently based on their skill levels and readiness to take on tasks, or coursework on how to manage people through results instead of "how they accomplish tasks." Many individuals may not have been taught these skills or been exposed to them previously, and they therefore will need help achieving this objective.

Level 3: What Needs to Change in Each Function

Lean Accounting Competencies

Lean Accounting may have significant differences from traditional accounting. Many organizations are shifting the theory, work, and results of the accounting group to better support continuous improvement efforts. Lean accounting would be seen in changes both inside and outside the function, as the accounting practices would be amended to match the flow and purpose of Lean.

For example, companies may change how they value inventory, how they track product costs, and how they measure performance in general. Lean accounting competencies would detail the skills and abilities needed to support a Lean environment, including business improvement tools, Lean theory, and the application and knowledge of how to modify accounting principles to match Lean principles. The transition in Lean accounting competencies is significant, and it requires accounting personnel to fully apply themselves to learning about Lean principles as they make significant changes to how financial information is recorded.

Some changes to accounting methods may result in what appears to be a "negative" effect on the financials, and those changes need to be fully understood in terms of the benefits and reasons for the changes. Similar to every aspect of business, accounting systems were designed with a high degree of waste built into the system. Lean is devoted to *uncovering all waste* and *removing barriers that keep waste hidden*. The accounting area of most organizations devoted to Lean principles have required a complete overhaul of financial reporting and methods to more fully record Lean processes (as opposed to the historical waste-driven approach).

Lean Human Resources Competencies

Many sections of this book lay out the skills and abilities needed for HR to support continuous improvement or a Lean environment. An organization needs to lay out a strategy for the skills required of HR to support the business strategy and culture. Skills of Lean HR would include a significant amount of general and specific business knowledge, coaching skills, and consulting skills.

I have steered each of my Lean HR groups towards improving their business skills, teaching them the financials of the business, and strengthening their coaching skills to the business leaders they provide consulting level support. Similar to other support functions in an organization, Lean HR needs to modify current structures to Lean principles.

Lean Information Systems Competencies

As another support function, information management or technology (IT) also needs to be changed to support leaner processes. Beginning with customer requirements, information systems need to be redesigned to more effectively meet the needs of newly created processes. The organizational strategy should clearly be reflected in IT priorities as well as removing waste from information system processes. The IT department needs to encourage participation in discussions about priorities, planning, and how to best support change initiatives.

Lean Quality Assurance Competencies

Quality assurance (QA) has tended to be focused on products and services delivered to the customer. In Lean environments, these functions can take on expanded roles as to how quality assurance can be applied in a broader context to all processes of the business as well.

For example, if there are critical problems facing a business, QA managers may come in to support local work groups in evaluating their process and looking for the reason the problem is happening to prevent it from happening in the future. This outside facilitation and support may help provide the structure needed to pause and reflect before lessons are forgotten.

The expanded role of QA to included continuous improvement is also part of providing a greater value to the organization. QA, in addition to HR, may also have important roles in training and modeling Lean principles, in terms of process management and sustainability in work flow, as well as effective problem solving. Continuous improvement cultures require significant integration of Lean principles into daily life, which QA can help deliver and monitor. The results of QA efforts, similar to HR, can be measured through improved business results.

Level 4: Creating the Gold Standard for Each Job

Once you have established all the other requirements for your organization, your leadership, and each function, you finalize the process by creating a "gold standard" for each job, which includes attention to those roles that have job specific competencies. A culture devoted to improvement will require that additional job responsibilities be added into all jobs and many roles will have specific improvement-related duties.

HR will then need to have the background and skills to coordinate establishing current behaviors as well as working with managers to develop plans to change people's roles. The change in each individual role is critical to culture change and to allowing people to utilize much more of their skills towards vastly improved results.

Customizing Needed Job Skills for Any Organization

Earlier in this chapter we reviewed how to build continuous improvement competencies into each job. Yet each organization has a unique approach to building its future, which must be taken into account to successfully implement these ideas. HR professionals need to ask questions of people in key leadership roles that help surface needs to build important skills into each job. Many leaders may not realize the impact that could be achieved by building skills with related results to job, which necessitates HR providing expertise in the methods and benefits of job development.

Begin with Organization-Wide Requirements

You can develop organization-wide competencies in a format that is aligned with your organization's culture and common language. After reviewing the specific continuous improvement competencies, your HR professionals can simply take the desired results and cultural objectives and reflect them in the job competencies. The following types of questions uncover what job competencies may be needed organization-wide to promote the behaviors that will achieve needed results:

1. What common behaviors or skills would best serve our business strategy?
2. Do job requirements need to be altered to reflect our organizational needs?
3. Do training requirements need to be altered to build needed skills?

Define What Is Important for All Leaders

Next, HR can help identify critical skills and capabilities of leadership as a significant opportunity for improved results. Using a process of facilitation, HR identifies and describes the leadership competencies needed to achieve the business strategy and cultural objectives in a language that will be accepted by the organization. This process would involve HR understanding the satisfaction with the current leadership as well as areas for improvement through these types of questions:

1. How are our leaders and the current leadership requirements achieving our business strategy? How are our leaders *not* delivering our strategic objectives?
2. How well are our leaders persuading or inspiring the attainment of our cultural objectives? How are they *not* supporting our desired culture?
3. Are needed leadership requirements currently reflected in job requirements?
4. Would our organization be improved by a better understanding of leadership requirements in terms of specific job skills and abilities?

Bring the Strategy into Each Function and Job

As internal consultants, HR professionals may be working in any area of the business and often do not work at an organization-wide level. Therefore, specific functional competencies may be an area of opportunity for an HR professional to partner with a particular internal customer. The functional competencies should be developed in a format that is aligned with your organization's culture and common language, as well as of the particular function. Consider using the following questions to uncover what job competencies may be needed organization-wide to promote desired behaviors:

1. How would function-specific strategies require needed behaviors to be achieved?
2. Are these behaviors currently reflected in our job requirements?
3. Are these behaviors reflected in the skill development for this function?

Customizing Skill Requirements Is a Dynamic Process

Once you know the answers to the questions above, Chapter 12 provides a process for building these competencies into actual job documentation (or modifying it to include new skills). However, the documentation is only the written component and does not reflect the dynamic process required to increase the standards of performance for your leaders or for any position in your organization. Putting a plan to enrich jobs into writing will not, by itself, change your organization. After you have identified what new skills are required, people need to be evaluated and given ways to build those new skills. Ensuring new avenues of accountability and coaching support are also important to demonstrating new skills.

CHAPTER 11 SUMMARY

KEY IDEAS

■ Business strategies may link to cultural elements and job competencies to help your organization attain the results you desire.

■ Competencies are skills and abilities needed for a job. Competencies are broken down into four levels that cover the organization, leadership or management across all functions, individual departments, and specific jobs.

■ Lean competencies in all four levels have similarities as well as distinct differences.

■ It is important to customize your approach to Lean HR with competencies to fit your unique business and accepted vocabulary in your actual environment.

STRATEGIC QUESTIONS FOR HR

1. What competencies are currently required in your organization for all jobs that support your strategy?_____

_____

_____

_____

_____

_____

_____

_____

2. How do the current competencies support or fail to support your Lean efforts? _____

_____

_____

_____

_____

_____

_____

_____

LEAN HR IMPLEMENTATION ACTIONS

1. Evaluate Lean requirements against your current skill requirements, beginning with *the organization-wide level:*
   - Review the current job description for a mid-level manager of your operation.
   - Evaluate how the current requirements relate to Lean competencies for leaders, as noted in this chapter.
   - List areas that changing most job content would benefit the operation and bring elements from organization-wide training into the daily work. _____

   _____

   _____

   _____

   _____

   _____

   _____

   - Have collaborative conversations with managers to identify specific changes that might help boost your organization's current improvement efforts with various members of management.
   - Read Chapter 12, which provides more details on how to finalize new job requirements for managers with Lean competencies built into the work.

2. Evaluate Lean requirements against your current skill requirements, now turning to *the leadership or management level:*
   - Review the current job description for a mid-level manager of your operation.
   - Evaluate how the current requirements relate to Lean competencies for leaders as noted in this chapter.
   - Look for areas where changing the manager's job content would benefit the operation and bring elements from training into the daily work. _____

   _____

   _____

   _____

_____

_____

_____

■ Have collaborative conversations with managers to identify specific changes that might help boost your organization's current improvement efforts with various members of management.

■ Again, review Chapter 12, which provides more details on how to finalize new job requirements for managers with Lean competencies built into the work.

3. Repeat these processes for every management role, each department, or specific jobs as necessary or helpful to your improvement efforts.

Chapter 12

Job Analysis for the Future

Chapter 11 reviewed how continuous improvement principles could be built into job content for all employees, managers, within functions, and for each individual job. This chapter provides a process for *documenting* job content, which is an important aspect of using job content to support other HR programs such as selection, training, performance management, compensation, and rewards. Documenting jobs is more than simply creating standard job descriptions; instead, it reveals *how your organizational culture can be reflected within individual jobs.*

The Importance of Documenting Job Content

Job documentation performs several functions, listed here and described in the following sections:

1. It establishes a basis of accountability for a preferred culture.
2. It provides a mechanism to reflect Lean principles in each role.
3. It provides a method to connect all HR programs to common elements.
4. It provides a model for improving job content to better meet organizational needs.

This information demonstrates how to make your organizational culture more than mere statements that are posted on a wall and are instead put into *action.*

Documenting Job Content Establishes a Basis for Accountability

What people are held accountable for, they accomplish. Yet many organizations have failed to create structures for holding people accountable for standard results or job activities. Job content documentation therefore creates a written record of the requirements that will optimize the talent of the organization through clear accountabilities.

I first learned this type of documentation from an organization that greatly increased the skills of each employee, which allowed the organization to grow its production with fewer employees and at a premium quality level. I then implemented (more than once) this type of a job content redesign, and I've always found it to be a way to design more skills and abilities into each job, so that people become clearer about new expectations and the underlying skills they need to build to perform their jobs.

Documenting Job Content Establishes a Basis for Applying Lean Principles

As discussed throughout this book, many organizations realize that improvement methods need to be more than discrete projects or programs. However, although many organizations have become clear about their desire to create a *culture* of improvement, it has not been obvious how it can be implemented. Building improvement skills, activities, and results into jobs creates a culture of improvement that will sustain itself. Job documentation involves applying the Lean competencies for the organization, as well as the leaders, to be added into specific job requirements.

I have used this job content approach to build new skills into jobs that added each phase of the work flow into each job as well as team-based problem-solving skills. Up until then, I had considered wanting people to work together as a team to be *preferred,* but not something we could *require.* Yet, as you might expect, those expectations that are loose and unspoken are mostly not subscribed to over time. Making team behaviors *standard work* created an environment where *how people solved problems* was as much a part of their work as making product each day.

Documenting Job Content Provides a Method to Link HR Programs

Job content documentation allows each core HR program to link to a common document as the basis for employee selection, training, development, performance management, recognition, and rewards. Chapter 13 details how organizations might approach these core HR programs differently to achieve strategic objectives and superior financial results. Typically (if not almost always), HR programs are designed separately from each other and only remotely link to one another. HR activities are able to be carried out without a strong design based on general expectations. For example, people get hired to meet a particular need, or someone wants to develop a new skill, so HR builds a program to meet that need; or it's the end of the year, so a new bonus program is designed for the following year.

However, when programs are developed at different times and places, it is usually not possible to have a clear system underlying the programs. By approaching each intervention as its own event with no clear link to an overall design, there is a *wasted* opportunity to gain the momentum that would be possible by *aligning* the programs. The goal of Lean HR is to have all HR programs aligned to underlying concepts to strengthen the cultural impact. Therefore, the job content documentation provides a basis to work from when implementing and working with core HR programs.

Documenting Job Content Provides a Model for Process Improvement of Jobs

The process of redesigning jobs benefits your organization because it requires you to consider what behaviors and key results you want to require for specific roles. One way to consider job design is as a type of process improvement for jobs. Similarly, the process involves creating a documentation of the "current condition" and then the proposed "future condition."

For example, a production worker might have a job description that states he or she:

■ Makes product;
■ cleans his or her area; and
■ works to certain quality specifications.

Additionally, this job could also include these functions:

■ Adding data to required reports;
■ Performing quality checks on his or her own product and recording their quality data; and
■ Participating in problem-solving teams and contributing ideas that help his or her area improve.

The documentation can be gathered in a document called a "Job Content Matrix," but the process itself holds considerable value.

Creating a Job Content Matrix

Table 12.1 is a generic example of job documentation that details enough specific information to guide all HR programs. A job matrix differs from a job description in that descriptions are primarily for recruitment purposes and even then they are often not meaningful in describing job duties. Developing a more advanced approach to analyzing job content, such as the matrix shown here, is required to first establish the best practice for a given job or role that is held by a number of people as well as to establish a basis to redesign job content against strategic objectives.

The matrix in Table 12.1 has three columns that detail separate aspects of a job which are then used to guide different HR related programs and as a guide to assessing current performance levels. I have often observed managers to find these matrixes quite illuminating in how they help them hold people accountable more effectively as well as support better problem solving for a wide range of performance issues. The matrix un-bundles a job description to provide a better understanding of all the components of a job, which helps you get a handle on the overall dynamics of the work, instead of a two-dimensional description. *While the Matrix examples show*

Table 12.1   Lean Culture Model: Job Content Matrix

Knowledge Requirements	Observable Behaviors	Required Results
Selection or training needs	*Training and/or performance systems*	*Rewards and/or recognition*
Possible selection criteria or associated training need	Specific behavior	Key results
Possible selection criteria or associated training need	Specific behavior	Key results
Possible selection criteria or associated training need	Specific behavior	Key results

clear line-ups between knowledge requirements, behaviors, and results, it is not at all necessary that there be the same amount of them on the page. Not every behavior links to a key result or a distinct knowledge requirement. On the other hand, some observable behaviors have more than one knowledge requirement or demonstrated result.

1. Knowledge requirement (selection and training programs). The first is the training or selection criteria that cannot be seen but are clearly needed by the person in order to perform specific tasks.
2. Activities to observe (training and performance systems). The second areas are the observable activities that are also areas we use to define training requirements and performance system structures.
3. Expected or required results (rewards and recognition programs). Last, we describe the job in terms of desired or required results. Results may provide opportunities for rewards and recognition or both.

Step 1: Documenting Observable Activities of Each Job

Instead of beginning with the far left column of "knowledge requirements," documenting job content begins with *observable behaviors*. When you're first documenting the current condition of a job in your organization, the matrix information is simply what you can observe during a current workday. Although you can group categories of activities in different ways, you need to focus on representing *the total picture* of any key activities. For example, you could group activities by timing (i.e., what portion of the shift each person worked) and/or functional areas (e.g., safety, quality, finance, people, team, etc.).

The activity portion of the matrix is a sentence description of the behavior itself. For example:

Ensures appropriate quantities of product are available for the beginning of the shift.

The level of detail is up to the designer, but it should be at a level of detail that links well with the key results and knowledge requirements of that job (described in the next paragraphs).

Step 2: Documenting Knowledge Requirements of Each Job

Knowledge requirements are obvious—and yet, they can be elusive. Although knowledge cannot be seen, it is traceable to performance and success. Documenting the knowledge requirements of each job is critical, so that employees are clear about what they need to know in order to perform their job tasks well.

For example, if you require an employee to conduct a quality check of his or her work by measuring the temperature of the product, the knowledge requirement would include knowledge of the quality check procedure and the meaning of particular results as the underlying information to complete the task properly.

In addition, the knowledge requirements provide a way to evaluate an employee's readiness to perform a job for either a training needs analysis or as part of a selection process. For example, once you have a list of the knowledge requirements, you can simply verify if a particular candidate or someone in the job knows everything needed to do the job. Any missing or weak areas that relate to knowledge can be supported by training plans.

You can also analyze performance problems against potentially missing knowledge components. I've also found that at times when a job isn't being done right, the problem lies in the lack of knowledge of a particular area. Based on the example just mentioned, if the quality check is not conducted properly, I found it important to then check if the person had been adequately trained to do the job and if not, we reinforced the issue with additional on-the-job education.

Simple questions that check for understanding can help identify if the underlying issue when performance is not up to standard may link to lack of knowledge.

Step 3: Documenting the Results Required of Each Job

Results need to be measured and visible. Here are just a few examples of results that are measureable and visible:

- Completed reports;
- stated production efficiency levels;
- costing standards;
- labor levels;
- achievement of quality standards; and
- safety performance.

Ensure that your matrix links required results to small groupings of activities. For example, you wouldn't have a required result that is a summary statement that "products are at standard quality levels." Instead, you would put a result of properly completed quality reports done at appropriate inter-vals as the visible measurable results.

The result might also include written evidence that changes are made to adjust production when quality results require adjustment. Problems in the workplace can be caused by a lack of clarity about required results, which may lead to difficulties with accountability. One of the greatest opportu-nities facing management teams today is to ensure that results are clear and visual whenever feasible (as discussed in Chapter 11). Another ben-efit of clarifying results is that people generally find it motivating to know where they need to focus, instead of being confused about standards of performance.

Begin with Entry-Level Management

Now that you know the basics of documenting jobs, let's review the steps you could take when developing a matrix for entry-level management. I have found starting with entry-level management is critical to forming the foundation of the type of workplace you want to create. As noted in Chapter 11, leaders who give work meaning create groups of people who embrace change. Managers or leaders who inspire and listen create groups of people who share new ideas and take on new challenges.

Table 12.2 reflects an example of a Leadership Job Matrix which might apply to most any mid-level management or supervisory role. Because front-line leaders create the environment in a workplace, I always start the Job Matrix design process with the lowest-level management role. I've also found that the first area of disconnect between what people are taught and then experience occurs when people are told they need to solve prob-lems, but their managers aren't congruent with that expectation and haven't adjusted their style accordingly. Therefore, start with defining the leaders you want in your organization. As mentioned, first start with observing their behavior. Don't just take a standard job description and work from there. I have always found it beneficial to truly watch over the course of a shift what the supervisors "do." Particularly, look at what the most effective supervisors "do" all day. This is often the beginning of establishing some best practices in the job matrix that will help other supervisors achieve better results by showing them what actual steps get the results they are required to achieve.

Table 12.2   Job Content Matrix: Lean Leadership Examples

People Management		
Knowledge Requirements	*Observable Behaviors*	*Required Results*
Coaching skills Job requirements to coach against	Coaching	Employees meet required standards for positions
	Constructive feedback	Consistent and fair treatment provided all employees
	Handling disciplinary procedures	Conduct addressed consistently and in a manner that protects the culture
Productivity		
Knowledge Requirements	*Observable Behaviors*	*Required Results*
Methods of production or service provision	Supervision of production or service provision	Productivity levels
Fact-based problem-solving methods Team-based problem solving when needed	Resolve production or service-related issues	Acceptable levels of defects Required productivity levels
System that feeds reports	Complete daily reports	Timely and accurate reports

Next, the process involves establishing the knowledge requirements and results for each item. Generally, developing this material requires asking more than one person what someone needs to know to do the tasks well and how given areas of responsibility are monitored for results. This process is generally done with more than one work content expert who currently does the job, paying closer attention to those with high levels of performance.

Once completed, the documentation is reviewed with a broad range of people currently doing a job to ensure that all components of the job have been gathered. Lastly, you should also review the documentation with the managers of the relevant area, to ensure that it meets the needs of the organization.

One staff member completes the documentation process and then reviews the material with other staff members to ensure completeness and consider insights from the process. After the process of gathering the information is complete, review each component of the job matrix before considering how to enlarge the job to meet changing needs and to reflect enlarged roles that are typical in Lean organizations.

Complete the Documentation through Teamwork

First, establish the precise job to be documented. Next, establish a group of people to obtain the information. As with all best practices or gold standards, choose carefully to work with people who seem to display much of what would be considered the desired characteristics, behaviors, and results.

Begin with documenting the job first on an action basis. Each action should be an observable behavior that anyone can see on a given day. As mentioned, the activities can be grouped chronologically, by topic or both.

Behaviors Provide Knowledge and Results

Once you have identified the behaviors of each job (which should fill up several pages), then you should go back and document, for each key behavior, what the knowledge or training requirements are that will support that behavior. Answer this question for each activity grouping:

> What does the person need to know to complete the job?

This information can be used to:

1. Develop recruiting requirements to establish areas that the organization desires not to have to train on the job.
2. Establish training requirements for job holders that will drive better behaviors and results.

3. Support performance problem analysis to establish if disappointing results may be linked to knowledge requirements that aren't met.
4. Help the coaching process by providing standards to evaluate proficiency to support the attainment of desired results.

Identify the Future Proposition for Jobs

After an initial draft of the job is documented as it is done currently, the continuous improvement process calls for another look at whether that job has been optimized. In general, after looking over the competencies discussed in Chapter 11, you may discover a job needs to reflect broader responsibilities that include problem solving, decision making, customer orientation, and developing leadership skills.

Think of this process as the redesign you might do of an organizational process but applied to job content instead. This is a way to build in Lean principles, tools, skills, and orientations into the fabric of the jobs on a day-to-day basis. The opportunity for optimization also entails more cross-training to other parts of the process.

Does this job content documentation optimize the role of the people who hold this job?

The Importance of a Lean Leader Matrix

For many organizations, developing a Lean leader matrix might be considered the documentation of standard work for leaders. Standard work, or specifications for work content, are obviously more typical for hourly positions and are not typically available for leaders. However, visionary leadership requires a Lean leader standard from which to work.

Once one level of Lean leader is established, which might be either a first-level supervisor or a manager of supervisors, then the work documentation can be edited much more easily and quickly because the basic elements of the job have been outlined. However, it also provides an important element in the design of the jobs to reflect how various levels of management are different in how they deliver results and perform job tasks. Standard work has become a well-accepted practice in Lean companies for production work, but it is still a developing concept for leaders. Yet how can you create visionary leadership without a roadmap for their development and performance?

Organizational Job Content Matrix

This chapter does not review how to create the job content for each job in the organization, so let's end this discussion with an overview of how to create organization-wide job content pages that can be customized for a particular job and level. Once the first managerial matrix is completed, the next matrix, shown in Table 12.3, is generally a matter of dialing up or down the level of leadership, team skills, and problem solving required in meeting the specific job. Also the job documentation can expand or contract based on desired scopes of various jobs. Similar to the process for creating a Leadership Job Matrix, an organization-wide matrix can be developed in a team formation and begin with the behavioral component of the work followed by links to knowledge requirements and demonstrated results. Once you have one non-managerial job completed with organization-wide competencies, it becomes relatively simple to create one for other job roles by adding job-specific and department-specific elements. I have often started this section with a production role that is not overly specialized and that is relevant to a relatively large number of the people. The over-arching objective of the design of the first organization-wide matrix is to create a vision for enlarged roles that likely include

Table 12.3   Job Content Matrix: Organization Wide

Knowledge Requirements	*Observable Behaviors*	*Required Results*
Selection or training needs	Training and/or performance systems	Rewards and/or recognition
Possible selection criteria or associated training need	Team-based problem solving	Department problems solved
Possible selection criteria or associated training need	Ensure perfect quality	Quality standards met
Possible selection criteria or associated training need	Participation	Required levels of suggestions

required customer focus, participation, problem solving, team work, and other new job duties. These enlarged roles are a key foundation for optimizing people and achieving cultural change.

As this section ends, Chapters 11 and 12 create a foundation for Section III that covers the four core HR programs for recruitment, training, performance management, and rewards. Most organizations do not have a formal process for implementing competencies, enlarging jobs, or fully documenting every facet of job performance. However, organizations devoted to cultures of continuous improvement are not fully served with a failure to strategically design their job structures.

Creating Evaluations Once a Matrix is Completed

Once a Job Matrix is approved by all interested parties, it is then implemented by developing some type of Evaluation Form (or checklist) which corresponds to each component of the Matrix. The Evaluation Form begins with demonstrated behaviors which are followed by the knowledge requirements and critical results. I have typically done the evaluations by having the employee perform a self evaluation while their manager completes one separately. The manager and the employee then meet to discuss where their viewpoints differ and seek to reach consensus on the final version of the Evaluation. The purpose of the evaluation process is to identify training gaps or other performance areas that need to be strengthened. The Evaluation Form helps an individual become more deeply familiar with the changes in their job's design so they can clarify next steps in their development and performance. Typically, I have seen organizations allow at least one or more years to close gaps reflected in the evaluation by charting detailed plans.

CHAPTER 12 SUMMARY

KEY IDEAS
- Documenting job content is a critical element of implementing a Lean culture.
- Job content documentation can be put into a matrix format that covers observable behavior, knowledge requirements, and critical results.

- Approaching job content documentation as an improvement process to optimize job content and expand jobs to achieve superior results is the real benefit of creating these documents.
- Evaluations against job content documentation provide a basis for assessing current talent and driving Lean HR strategies for improvement.

STRATEGIC QUESTIONS FOR HR

1. Would your continuous improvement efforts be enhanced if the job content for leaders better reflected Lean competencies? _____

_____

_____

_____

_____

2. Would your culture be stronger if the job content for your leaders or other positions reflected elements of your desired culture? _____

_____

_____

_____

_____

3. Will the jobs in your organization, as they are currently designed, achieve your business strategy? _____

_____

_____

_____

_____

LEAN HR IMPLEMENTATION ACTIONS

1. Examine your job descriptions for relevance to your continuous improvement efforts. Do you see opportunities to add job requirements that would support your cultural objectives? *Note if your descriptions could be improved by separating knowledge requirements and key results from the job activities.* _____

_____

_____

_____

_____

_____

_____

2. What changes can your organization make to expand on your job requirements to challenge more of people's abilities and improve your results? *Consider whether you would start with leadership roles and broader groups of people.* _____

_____

_____

_____

_____

_____

_____

STRATEGIES FOR ALIGNING YOUR HR PROCESSES

V

Section V contains the most significant components of how Lean or continuous improvement is built into the most traditional HR processes that drive how people work throughout your organization. Chapter 13 covers how developing a plan for job competencies and redesigning job content will end up influencing recruitment training, performance management and rewards. This chapter also covers how these processes need to be redesigned in general to support Lean implementations or continuous improvement cultures.

Chapter 14 will cover a five-year plan to implement changes to your current HR processes to support your desired culture changes and the successful implementation of your business strategies. Chapter 14 reviews how using a five-year plan is a helpful tool in phasing in changes in a methodical and well paced manner.

Chapter 13

Linking the Four Core HR Processes to the Overall Business Strategy

Chapters 11 and 12 focused on job content and the documentation of job analysis to enlarge jobs in order to optimize the abilities of your people. Job content and analysis are the underpinnings for how an HR strategy is executed through core HR processes against the overall business objectives and goals of the organization. Therefore, this chapter reviews the four core HR processes:

1. Recruitment
2. Training
3. Performance management
4. Rewards

   Each of these core HR processes can significantly impact the results of your organization, so each is a potential strategic lever. You might be accustomed to thinking about each of the core processes *separately*, so this may be the first time you have considered them *in comparison* to each other, in terms of which one is the best suited to achieve your strategic business results. By considering each of the above processes as a strategic lever, you can highlight how they can be designed for impact—not just as a reaction to immediate needs or rooted in past practices.

HR Processes Can Be Strategic Levers

HR processes operate as strategic levers when used as powerful tools for significant impact, but they require good design and execution. First, consider the typical impact of an organization that simply hires people; then consider one that achieves superior results by hiring the *right* people through top-grade recruitment and selection techniques, followed by a "best-in-class" orientation in an all-out effort to hire individuals with skills and attitudes that match the organization's culture. The latter is an organization that understands the impact of people in the achievement of their goals and seeks to optimize their workforce from the very beginning.

A strategic lever reflects a possible source of leverage to create the desired effect or impact. An HR strategic lever is one that allows an organization to impact people or their behavior in a way that dramatically impacts results. This chapter reviews each of the core processes in terms of how excelling at what will produce superior results, but first we consider why you need to excel at *only one* of the core HR processes as your *primary* strategic lever.

Excelling at One Primary Process Is Enough

Organizations need to focus on only one of the core HR processes as the leading strategic lever because they link together, so one strong lever can influence the others. Although any of the core processes can be designed to support the business strategy, it's recommended that only one be chosen as the key strategic lever, for two reasons:

1. First, focusing on only one allows the HR department to concentrate its resources, which helps ensure that excellence is achieved in at least *one* of the core processes.
2. Second, it is unnecessary to excel at all four processes, because they feed into each other. For example, if an organization focuses on selecting only the best candidates, then the need to train and develop those employees will be significantly reduced. By the same token, if a company hires average individuals, it might choose to excel at *training and development,* which will optimize the work of those employees.

In addition to identifying what the implications are for each of the four primary core HR processes in terms of its strategic opportunity, this chapter reviews how continuous improvement can be designed into the entire HR system, including how to use benchmarking to achieve higher levels of excellence. Table 13.1 shows how each core program is a strategic advantage as the focal point of the HR strategy as well as the corresponding disadvantages of making that particular program the focal point.

Better HR Processes through Benchmarking

A discussion of improvement would not be complete without a review of *benchmarking*. Improvement efforts can be greatly enhanced with benchmarking to generate fresh ideas and utilize a breadth of experiences outside the company. Much can be gained when you (and your team) reach out to other organizations that have particularly strong core HR processes, and then bring those ideas back to your organization and make them your own. Not only is this practice rich with rewards, but it is also highly energizing for your team members as well.

You should identify particular areas of interest for benchmarking and look for companies that have reputations for best practices. To locate a possible benchmarking site, you can ask other professionals in your area for recommendations for what they consider best in class. Vendors can be another strong source for best practices. For example, if you contact a selection testing company to look for best-practice organizations in the area of employee selection processes, you may find particularly strong practices. Be prepared to travel to get to best-in-class sites, if your goal is to see the best and not limit yourself to a local contact. You may also want to contact companies that present their best practices at either HR conferences or Lean conferences to find companies that may be possible benchmarking sites for HR programs.

Consider bringing a team of people with you to any benchmarking meeting, and each person should be prepared with questions he or she wants to ask during the visit. Most organizations, if they are not direct competitors, are willing to share their materials and in-depth practices as a matter of goodwill. Be sure to follow up any benchmarking visit with a proper note of gratitude, and include comments on what you have learned if possible. I've often presented a gift from my organization that is an offering of our product line, and I've often received one in exchange.

As we now consider each of the four core processes, think about how you might locate best practices in your effort to improve HR by seeing what other companies are doing.

Table 13.1 The Four Core HR Processes as Strategic Levers

Core HR Processes or Strategic Levers	Advantages of Leading with This Lever	Disadvantages of leading with This Lever
Recruitment		
• *Recruiting candidates* • *Selecting the right people* • *Orientation of new employees or people into new jobs*	Eliminates some of the cost and other resources required to train people after they have been hired. Best used as the primary lever in a start-up organization.	Tends to be most helpful with new hires, so organizations that have less hiring will not find this lever as effective.
Training and development		
• *Training for management* • *Training for all employees* • *Development plans and programs to build management/leadership skills*	A considerable volume of training materials are readily available to build skills into an existing workforce.	Requires extensive resources and follow up. Many organizations lack the skills and understanding for the follow up that is needed to receive the benefits of training.
Performance management		
• *Commonly referred to as "standard work" to establish clear expectation* • *May include standard work for leaders/managers*	Can be a stronger strategic lever to produce improved performance than training because the focus is on the execution or actual application of skills with required results.	Additional skills may need to be built into jobs that performance management or standard work will not create by itself.
Recognition and rewards		
• *Reinforcement of behaviors through recognition* • *Ability to incentivize behavior through rewards*	It is a primary lever, typically seen with some types of gain-sharing programs that drive behavior, not just reward results.	Pay systems can easily create morale problems if there are unmet expectations. In addition, expectations are difficult to meet over time for any program design.

Strategic Lever Number One: Recruitment
"An Often-Missed Opportunity"

Recruitment actually involves three processes.

1. **Recruiting potential employees:** The recruitment process begins with the identification of candidates and ends where the selection process begins.
2. **Selecting the right employees:** Selection is a process that generally begins with a pool of candidates and defines the steps that would best support picking the right candidates for a continuous improvement culture.
3. **Orienting new employees into the organization:** On-boarding begins with the hiring of a candidate and follows the first 90 to 180 days of orienting new employees.

These recruitment-related processes all link together, creating your success in hiring the right people into your organization and making sure they get started in understanding your culture from the beginning. I have found that recruitment is often not seen as an opportunity to impact overall results based on the quality of people hired or how people are oriented to their work. Yet the first place you can begin to impact your talent pool is by creating meaningful filters which only allow the right types of skills and abilities into your workplace. Once you hire people, it's also critical that you convey important messages at the outset, when people are most focused on knowing what's expected of them and on their role in the bigger picture.

Start with Looking for Improvement-Oriented Leaders

Following are some ideas about how to locate talented people who are familiar with Lean principles, continuous improvement cultures, and the importance of demonstrating superior results over time.

Database searches: Seek out candidates by searching through databases of candidates using words like "continuous improvement" or "Lean." Other phrases like "root cause analysis" can also be helpful. Finding qualified candidates who are familiar with Lean principles does require some type of selection process to weed out those who know only the language, as opposed to those who truly know how to achieve Lean results.

Lean recruiters: A specific niche of recruiters has developed with a particular focus on Lean, and these recruiters can refer individuals who have particular skills in improvement cultures and Lean principles.

Professional associations: Several professional associations include material on Lean principles. Here are three examples:

- *The Association of Manufacturing* (http://www.ame.org) is a not-for-profit association that is devoted to companies learning from each other in the interest of continuous improvement. Membership fees are nominal and provide access to other members who have experience with optimizing people through leadership, participation, problem solving, and focusing on the customer. This association has an annual conference and regional events and conferences on both Lean concepts in general and different particular areas of interest, such as Lean accounting or supply chain management.
- *The Society of Mechanical Engineers* (SME) offers Lean certification; information can be found on its Web site at http://www.sme.org/certification.
- *The American Society of Quality* (ASQ) also has material for a Lean enterprise at http://ASQ.org/le as well as other pertinent information.

Use Tools to Select the Right People

Organizations find it well worth their while to recruit the best quality of candidates possible to improve performance. "Best quality" may not mean that the people are the smartest or the fastest, but that they are a good fit for the culture you want to create. Therefore, quality candidates need to be defined by what is important to *your* organization.

The set of selection questions shown in Table 13.2 reflects how you can use questions that are based on behaviors to identify the right types of traits for any organizational hire. You can customize the behavioral questionnaire to your organization's needs, which also allows the interview process to be tailored more specifically to establishing how well matched an individual is to your organization. The answers to the questions in Table 13.2 are rated as "+" when the response is specific and a direct link to the desired skill or cultural characteristic. The answer is rated "−" when the response is distinctly out of alignment with the desired skill or characteristic. The answer is "Neutral" or 0 when the response is not distinctly positive or negative. You might also use rating scales of 1 to 10 to better quantify the results with multiple rates or candidates; for example:

Table 13.2   Sample Behavioral Questions for Lean Organizations

Sample Questions	*Rating: +; Neutral; or –* *(Score 1–10)*
Question 1: How do you view the role of the customer? *Evaluate answers for concrete example(s) of making customers a priority.*	
Question 2: Have you participated in making an improvement at work? What was your role? What did you learn? *Evaluate answers for concrete example(s) of demonstrated achievement and interest in topic and learning.*	
Question 3: Have you ever made a suggestion that was implemented to improve something in the environment? *Evaluate answers for concrete examples of participation and improvement.*	
Question 4: Give an example of a problem that you solved at work. How did you solve it? *Evaluate answers that show fact-based problem solving and willingness to identify problems.*	
Question 5: What is the process you worked on in your last job? *Evaluate answers that reflect understanding of processes.*	
Question 6: What measurements have you seen displayed in the workplace? Have you worked towards goals before? *Evaluate answers for demonstration of visual management.*	
Question 7: What is your own personal definition of leadership? *Evaluate answers for positive impressions of leadership.*	

- A rating of 7 to 10 would be a positive result.
- A rating of 0 to 3 would reflect a negative result.
- A rating of neutral would be in the range of 4 to 6.

I've used this approach to focus the interview on the right issues and evaluate candidates better against each other.

Although all hires are important, leadership is especially crucial to the creation and maintenance of a high-performing culture, which is why organizations often take extra measures to select leaders with a propensity to best inspire their teams to perform. These are not leaders who *mandate* action; instead, they are leaders who *coach* people to better performance in a way that fosters high morale. Therefore, the selection process for these individuals needs to be robust, in order to identify individuals who are most able to inspire their teams. Table 13.3 shows how behavioral questions can be designed that focus on organization-wide needs as well as the type of leadership needed for an engaged workforce.

Many tests and tools are available that help organizations select leaders for continuous improvement cultures. I've used tests by Wonderlic to handle the selection of broad groups of employees. I've tended to use outside resources to support the selection of managers, and those resources use a wide variety of testing tools. Using a reputable employee selection/testing company enables an organization to select tests that can help shed light on personality and management styles most able to support an environment that looks to optimize human potential.

Try Outside Resources for Selecting the Right Leaders

Because identifying leaders may be difficult at best, you might consider outsourcing this job to a professional firm. Some industrial psychologists specialize in evaluating managers to assess their ability to support a participative environment and to be able to create other leaders (in addition to being able to lead themselves).

Outsourcing selection can be relatively inexpensive, or it can cost several thousand dollars. Yet for many organizations that truly realize the value of this task, the cost of recruiting is a small fraction of the risk involved in bringing in the wrong leaders. I have found that paying for support to have higher-quality hires is more than offset by the cost of hiring people who are not suited to our culture. Some would say the firm will help prevent mistakes, more than it can forecast someone's ability to lead these important cultures.

Table 13.3   Sample Behavioral Questions for Lean Leaders

Sample Questions	Rating: +; Neutral;or– (Score 1–10)
1. Give an example of a problem you have had with a customer: how did you handle it? *Evaluate answers for concrete example(s) of making customers a priority.*	
2. Give an example of an improvement you have made in the past that was significant and a measurable result was achieved. How did you approach identifying and implementing the improvement? Who was involved? Is it still in place? *Evaluate answers for concrete example(s) of demonstrated achievement of material gains, use of employee involvement, use of Lean or repeatable methodology, and whether improvement was sustainable.*	
3. If you were to have employees participate here at our company, how would you go about that? *Evaluate answers for concrete examples of processes that use participation that are daily, repeatable, and sustainable.*	
4. How would you solve a problem that needs your attention and involves several departments? *Evaluate answers that show fact-based problem solving using teams across departments to solve problems.*	
5. What processes have you managed in the past? *Evaluate answers that reflect understanding of processes and orientation to create repeatable, sustainable processes that achieve desired results.*	
6. Give an example of how you've displayed results for employees to see: What were the results? *Evaluate answers for demonstration of visual management.*	
7. What is your own personal definition of leadership? *Evaluate answers for characteristics such as motivation of people, supporting staff, working through influence, positive momentum, and other desired characteristics.*	

Allow the Team to Select Its Own Members and Leader

Because the concept of leadership is so important, teams are often involved in making hiring decisions. Continuous improvement cultures may use team-based interviewing, because of their focus on teamwork. Teams that drive results together generally prefer to have some choice in who is added to their group, including their leader. Teams also are able to add considerable insight into the hiring process because they provide several viewpoints.

Team interviews can establish the tone of continuous improvement culture from the time a candidate first meets your organization. The sample questionnaires in Tables 13.2 and 13.3 are great tools for teams to use when interviewing, to compare the candidates' answers.

Evaluate Your Organization's Current Leadership

One feature I have repeatedly encountered in high-performing organizations is the idea that you should *reselect* people into the roles they play once you have designed changes into job requirements. In other words, the people who were originally considered as qualified for a job may not possess the right qualifications for the future.

The process of reselecting people who already are working in positions takes considerable planning and diplomacy to handle it well and prevent significant morale problems that can last for years to come. As you might think, informing people that in the future they may not be right for the job they currently hold, because there has been a change in direction, creates anxiety for most people. The process for establishing the new qualifications needs to be concrete and well documented. In addition, every effort should be made to allow people to grow into the qualifications before they are either put into other jobs or asked to leave your organization. This approach is not for everyone, but I've seen it successfully create radically improved results by ensuring the leadership in place is better able to coach and inspire their teams to higher levels of performance.

The role of leadership is a significant component of the success and failure of any organization, so considering the competency of the individuals holding those roles and making changes if necessary to achieve your desired culture may be very important. Successful organizational change begins with the people holding leadership roles. HR has an important role to support the organization in defining the leadership characteristics that will best support the efforts needed to create a continuous improvement culture. This issue is critical because having the wrong leaders in place is generally a deal breaker: in other words, your organization really can't be successful if you don't have the right leaders.

Senior leaders or the ownership of an organization can issue an announcement that continuous improvement will be the future of the company and that employees' ideas are important for getting better results. However, if the supervising leaders pay no attention to continuous improvement or having employees participate, then it becomes clear that the change is not real. The reverse is also true: having the right leadership in place will generally bring the desired results to your customers and your business. Since leadership is so important, it's critical that a process be in place to set the criteria, adequately evaluate people against those criteria, and ensure that mechanisms are in place for how to deal with people who do not meet them.

Strong Cultures Demand Strong Orientations

Strong cultures demand that employees be given a message about working and living in a particular culture from the very beginning of their employment. Lack of attention to highlighting organizational culture leads to average (or worse) results. For an organization to obtain above-average results from its new hires, it needs to truly consider what messages are being given to people.

First, you need to determine the critical elements that on-boarding needs to begin to reinforce, and try to think out of the box about what types of on-boarding activities would support those messages. On-boarding can entail any number of activities, such as:

- Presentations by a variety of internal departments
- The necessary training to begin work
- Tours of the facility
- Working with buddies to learn more about daily life in the organization
- A presentation on policies described in the employee handbook

Generally, you should begin by working from what is important to your organization's particular culture, then design your orientation process to give employees critical messages about what matters. People will likely be too new to experience much of any real training, but it is imperative to display concepts of value from the beginning. Each of the Lean principles may be featured in a continuous improvement culture. How might the on-boarding process drive those messages?

Here are some ideas on how to educate new employees about each goal that's important to you:

- *Customer focus* might include introductory material for new employees that describes your organization's top 10 customers, with complete profiles and other information that can make your customers real. This tells a candidate or a new hire that *your customers are important.*

■ *Sustained improvements* might include a review of your organization's progress in the last year and areas you've identified for improvement. New employees might go through a mini-simulation to reflect how improvement thinking will be prevalent in your organization.

■ *Participation* might include a way for newcomers to provide input on what they notice in the organization within the first week, which sets the tone up front.

■ *Team-based factual problem solving* might be highlighted in the orientation material, with pictures of improvement teams and the results of their efforts.

■ *Visible measurements* might include an orientation to the measurements in a manner that ensures the new hires truly understand the purpose and information behind the metrics.

■ *Leadership* might include people in a range of leadership roles providing motivational messages about how they want to support people's success and how they are there to help.

Strategic Lever Number Two: Training and Development
"Unless It Adds Value, It's Often a Waste of Resources"

This section reviews the theory and methods that have been developed in the area of training related to Lean or continuous improvement, how training must be carefully designed to add value, and how training should be implemented to align with strategic objectives. This discussion begins with how job content can be documented (as described in Chapter 12), including how Lean principles can be designed into each job within an organization.

Standard Work or Knowledge Requirements Create a Basis for Training Needs

The format for job documentation establishes the outline for standard work for managers, including the training requirements for specific jobs. Job documentation does not cover the details of standard work for specific production-type jobs. However, standard work of all types is intended to support better training that efficiently reduces variations that hurt quality and productivity. Done well, standard work also alleviates stresses for people because they will know precisely what is involved in work; standard work also creates motivation to improve results through a comprehensive work process.

Lean principles can be built into jobs (as shown in the examples of job documentation in Chapter 12) to reflect precisely what training is required to support people who need it. Table 13.4 provides an outline of commonly provided training in Lean implementations or cultures. If your organization doesn't have any training documentation, you would begin with evaluate the training needs of your organization and then develop long-term training plans.

Ensure Training Adds Value

Training often lacks any real, clear direction or required outcomes. Training needs to add value, or it is simply a waste of time and money. Waste also comes from a lack of the follow up required to support desired results.

> **If you think of training as a process, it should begin with an identified training need and end with the actual demonstrated behavior at a required level or result.**

The most common problems arise when organizations provide training that either isn't linked to a clear strategic need or fails to deliver the desired behaviors and related results. For training to add value, it must also link to the organization's overall strategy.

For example, I've seen many HR departments provide training for supervisors or leadership that they have designed apart from the strategic objectives of the organization. As the training is conducted, the departments involved will often fail to attend, or they resist the time away from their work to complete the training. This is the first sign that training has no clear value to the individuals, when they don't see the value in putting their time into the skill building.

In general, having people complete a few hours or even several hours of training will not necessarily change any behavior or result. In fact, changing behaviors or developing new ones is an extremely complex and difficult process. For example, I've participated in attempting to train many beginning supervisors in coaching and supervisory skills. Many people in the class leave the training a bit confused and often the areas of weakness are

Table 13.4   Common Training for Continuous Improvement or Lean Organizations

Training	Description	Purpose
Team training	Focus on skills that support teamwork, including leadership, facilitation, and membership roles.	Supports team-based problem solving and general process orientation across departments.
Leadership training	Skills include coaching, constructive feedback, employee engagement, visual management, and developing leaders.	Develops skills for people in managerial roles as well as informal leadership roles.
Waste 101	Basic tools and methods for understanding and identifying waste.	Provides fundamentals for team to begin to see waste and learn ways to remove waste.
Problem solving	Fundamentals including stating the problem, using facts to understand root causes, and methods for implementing effective changes.	Supports problem-solving skills.
Value stream mapping	Process for laying out current steps and possible future steps within a process.	Provides method for examining current practices in a team format and identifying changes for future improvements.

still present after 20 hours of training (even if it takes place over several weeks). The issue is that many people are having particular problems, for which they require one-on-one support to overcome or improve upon. Training is often conducted for the larger group, with little focus on individual struggles. People are often embarrassed about areas they need to improve and do not share in an open classroom what they struggle to learn. The solution to this problem is in providing one-on-one support to people well after the training is conducted, in a manner that is tailored to their individual needs.

Certainly, HR has an important role in understanding what is required to make training effective. HR can assist in identifying clear objectives and thorough follow-up plans and can ensure coaching and accountability are in place for successful training results.

Finally, although you *can* send employees for training either within the workplace or outside, it's usually better to conduct training internally. HR departments can at least coordinate these efforts, even if some of the training is done externally.

Connection to Strategy and Results

Your training should be linked to your organization's strategy. Companies may have either no training or may be conducting only minimal training (either because minimal training is legally required or because minimal training is all that historically has been performed). First-line supervisory training is an example of training commonly provided by organizations.

However, this approach to training can really prevent HR from performing the strategic role possible in relation to training. Table 13.5 shows a needs assessment interview form that can be used as a basis to ask and answer the critical questions to develop training programs that are not a waste of resources, but a real support for cultural initiatives. I've used the questions shown in Table 13.5 to help develop training processes or systems that fully meet business needs instead of operate as "quick hits" with little effect. The assessment should be designed to ensure there is a full understanding of the objectives involved and how the training needs to be targeted to deliver critical results.

Strategic Lever Number Three: People Thrive on Accountability
"The Great Controversy over the Role of Performance Management"

Some Lean or quality theories are avidly against performance management because of the possible negative effect on morale, which hurts the broad engagement needed to identify problems and optimize the impact of each person. Yet most organizations have performance management programs. This section examines possible controversies over whether performance reviews support broad employee engagement and addresses what performance management system would best develop a Lean culture.

Table 13.5   Needs Evaluation Interview Form for Training Assessment

1.	What are the critical issues facing the business?
2.	What are the critical strategies for the business?
3.	What are the long-term cultural objectives?
4.	How might training support these issues?
5.	What types of skills or behaviors would the training be expected to change?
6.	How could changes in behavior be measured?
7.	What types of follow up could support changes in behavior?
8.	What types of coaching would be required for the change in behavior?
9.	How would training results link to day-to-day accountabilities?
10.	Do the coaches or people who are holding trainees accountable need training themselves?

This section also describes other aspects of performance management, including standard work, which has become a widely used tool to better lay out expectations, and ensures performance is closely managed. We next discuss visual management and other performance management systems that ensure feedback to employees is quick and provides a basis for improvement instead of evaluating people on a subjective sense. We will review the use of 360° feedback programs as a tool to support changes to how leaders need to perform a different role in the participatory culture. Lastly, this section discusses the appropriate timing of performance management as well as the use of this strategic lever as the leading HR program.

The Downside of Performance Management Systems

The topic of *psychological safety* was first introduced as a leadership competency in how people manage in a continuous improvement culture. It encompasses what people need to feel safe or comfortable enough to share ideas, take risks, contribute more, and be fully engaged in their work. There are at least three critical concerns with performance feedback systems in general:

1. They tend to follow a bell curve rating, which leaves many people feeling they are average or even less-than-average employees.
2. Many individuals who participate in these systems lack the skills to handle performance feedback in a manner that maintains their relationships.
3. Many performance feedback systems are developed in a manner that limits, rather than expands, people's sense of potential and contribution.

Let's look at each of these concerns.

Concerns regarding using a bell curve rating. Starting with the issue of the bell curve, many organizations are philosophically founded on the idea that it is important to either rank employees literally or at least give people some type of a rating. Whether the ratings have three, five, or seven options, the emphasis is on how to let each individual know how he or she rates or ranks.

The problem with this approach is that it generally motivates a much smaller portion of the organization than the much larger group that ratings actually *demotivate*. Using the bell curve as an example, how many people would be demotivated if told they are average to below-average workers? There has been a false assumption that people wouldn't mind being told they are average, and that people who rate below average ought to be told they are below average, so that they can improve. If the process is demotivating, does it really help people improve?

Concerns regarding poor feedback. When the bell curve is combined with poor feedback skills, they both contribute to concerns with maintaining employee engagement. Therefore, the topic of performance management is fraught with opportunity to destroy relationships and motivation. Why? The process of feedback can be positive, but typically many of the individuals giving feedback lack the skills to do so in a manner that enriches relationships and improves productivity. For example, I have seen managers give negative feedback without any specific examples, leaving an employee wondering about the meaning of the feedback. I've often had managers tell someone that "you are not good with numbers" or "you are bad with people" which is interpreted as a label of the person, instead of directing attention to desired changes in behavior. Therefore, some people say it would be better to not have performance management systems than to risk the wide range of demotivating situations that come from these common exercises.

Feedback systems are limiting. Most written materials that are used for feedback provide simple categories and ratings with a few comments. These systems are limiting in that they narrow the person's view of their work and abilities. If the goal of a Lean culture is to expand the use of people's capabilities, performance management systems need to be redesigned to have each person, and their manager, to seek answers to the following questions.

- What am I capable of doing in my work that I'm not doing now?
- What are areas would I like to perform better?
- Where have I held myself back?
- What would I like to do more of to contribute to our organization?
- What problems could I work to solve?
- How could I closer to my customer(s)?
- How effective are the performance indicators I how I'm doing? Could my key results be more visual to be more effective?
- What types of support do I need to make changes to contribute more to my organization?

The Upside of Performance Management Systems

On the other hand, much can be said for the positive outcomes possible from giving people feedback on their performance. The absence of individual feedback might lead people to feel unimportant or not worthy of individual time with their supervisor. Therefore, the upside is that people feel a sense of recognition from the process.

Therefore, performance management systems should address how to best handle feedback in a manner that increases morale. This is not to say that managers should give people only positive feedback and not say anything critical. This is a matter of ensuring each person feels uniquely seen and able to contribute his or her personal skills to the work environment. It is also a matter of ensuring the feedback is given in a manner that is supportive. Last, it is a matter of ensuring the process actually helps people contribute more, not less. Table 13.6 shows how feedback differs in a traditional work environment, which focuses on blame, and a Lean environment, which focuses instead on accountability.

HR has an important role in ensuring accountability is in place for all employees in a manner that is effective. Accountability is fundamentally a basis for setting expectations and then following up on how well the individual accomplished the expectations. Although it is simple to describe,

Table 13.6 Feedback Emphasizing Blame versus Accountability

Culture of Blame	*Culture of Continuous Improvement*
Who did it?	Which process is involved?
Who is to blame?	Who is responsible for the process?
	Who are all the people who affect the process that are involved in an issue?
	Is the person responsible clear about this issue?
Who needs to be disciplined to ensure this never happens again? (Focus on past)	What can the people responsible do differently in the future? (Focus on future.)
Assumes people do not care.	Assumes people care.
Assumes people make mistakes due to carelessness or negligence.	Assumes people make mistakes due to a range of people-related processes that can be improved.
Assumes mistakes often repeat and are unavoidable.	Assumes mistakes are avoidable through well-designed processes.
Surfacing problems can lead to penalties or consequences. Disclosing errors is discouraged.	Surfacing problems is critical to error-proof process. Disclosing errors is encouraged.

it is quite difficult to establish a sufficient level of expectation that people can follow.

By nature, people want to know what is expected of them. This requires much more than a job description or a set of annual goals. Setting expectations requires giving employees a clear sense of direction, priorities, and outcomes that are expected over specific timeframes. The more common the work role is in the organization or the greater the amount of flexibility each person has in his or her contribution, the more challenging is the task of setting expectations.

Standard Work Creates a Baseline for Performance Feedback

The matrix in Chapter 12 is one approach to creating standard work for managerial-level positions as well as other jobs. Establishing standard work is not only a way to train people to do jobs in a uniform manner, it also provides a method to manage performance against clear requirements. As a performance management tool, standard work ensures expectations are properly set so that there is a point of reference for feedback systems. I have found standard work for supervisors to be hugely helpful in creating clear work processes to improve performance and the quality of production and related processes. Standard work establishes best practices for many supervisors with similar positions, which is often overlooked as an opportunity for improvement.

Visual Performance Management Systems

Visual management systems, which are an important tool of Lean work environments, are clearly a performance management system that provides immediate feedback to people about their work. People might describe much of their time at work in vague terms as to how effectively they are performing. Visual standards provide immediate feedback on key results to speed up responses to issues and improve performance over time. The purpose of performance-based systems is (obviously) to improve performance. Yet most programs provide feedback annually, semiannually, or monthly. Providing important feedback by the hour or day certainly speeds up learning processes and adjustments to obtain better results.

An example could be a board in a production room that gives an hourly reading on output levels and notes quality problems and any shortages in raw materials for later analysis. This board is viewed by all employees in a particular area and allows them to have a solid basis for knowing their performance levels throughout the day. I have seen boards used to report quality concerns, safety issues, and customer issues in a manner that is highly visible to all people who need that feedback to guide their performance. This technique is well proven to improve performance by simply ensuring performance feedback is direct, timely, and focused on the most important features of the work. Some organizations have even replaced annual review programs for production workers with systems that provide feedback on a daily basis.

Use of 360° Feedback Programs

A common program found in high-performing cultures is the use of 360° feedback systems. In a 360° feedback system, individuals obtain feedback from their managers, peers, and direct reports. One of the purposes of this type of feedback program is to ensure people are truly aware of the level of support they do or don't provide to their direct reports. Only through this type of system would many organizations have a mechanism for some people to give feedback. In an environment that has an inverted triangle view of management, having a feedback process that runs all around makes sense. Yet this process can be difficult and troublesome for people who are not accustomed to this type of feedback and need support in how to take the feedback and make important changes.

Strategic Lever Number Four: Recognition and Rewards
"Most Over- and Underestimated HR Process"

The discussion of rewards includes both financial and nonfinancial recognition. Let's begin with nonfinancial recognition as a foundation for creating an effective rewards program. This section also examines how recognition can positively reinforce desired behaviors. Also, keep in mind that financial rewards are a form of recognition. Continuous improvement cultures reinforce behaviors that support the corresponding culture elements. You can easily customize the overall approach to whatever behaviors you want increased through recognition or awards. We'll also review how financial recognition is a stronger form of recognition, which can be considerably more dangerous if not focused correctly. Generally speaking, rewards can be a more powerful *demotivator* than a motivator.

The Power of Recognition

Recognition can play an enormous role in motivating people to work towards goals and exhibit more desired behaviors. Generally, it is more common to believe recognition must be financial in nature, yet the opposite is often true. Ideally, recognition includes an acknowledgment of a specific behavior or contribution and the benefit it had on the work environment. I have often heard employees lament in a training session that they only wish their managers would mention the things they do *right*—instead of what they do wrong. People will comment that they want to know what daily activities can make a difference. Yet most managers will confess that they seem to feel most motivated to comment on work performance when something is wrong.

Equally true is that people respond positively to just being told they've handled something well. How do you feel when someone unexpectedly acknowledges your work or effort? I often teach this principle to managers by having them remember a time that someone recognized them and how it made them feel and how it affected their work. By remembering their own experience, managers realize they need to recognize others more often. Employees commonly remark that they hunger to have more simple recognition of their contribution and require less in the way of financial rewards.

Start with Desired Behaviors

Developing a clear approach to recognition begins with clarifying the behaviors you want to see or to grow. Therefore, HR can work with supervisors and managers to establish the desired behaviors they need in their areas. Going back to Chapter 11 on competencies, managers need to become clear on an appropriate level about what they want to recognize.

For example, if teamwork is a core competency for your organization, then it would make sense to recognize team work behaviors on a broad basis. As desired behaviors are established, supervisors and managers need to actively reinforce them during the work day in a way that promotes that behavior for the person being reinforced, as well as others.

I've typically taught supervisors to make sure they publicly acknowledge the behaviors they want to *grow* so that others understand these are the ways to be affirmed and do a good job. People are hard-wired to want to be successful. Put a lot more time into finding ways for people to feel successful everyday—not just every once in a while.

A Recognition Review

One way to assess potential opportunities for increasing or improving recognition is to do a recognition summary, such as the example shown in Table 13.7. Although the summary example focuses on the cultural elements of a continuous improvement culture, any set of elements could be placed in the first column and then evaluated as to the methods for recognition that exist for that element.

Financial Reward Systems

In addition to nonfinancial recognition, companies often choose to explore how to modify their financial reward systems to reinforce the attainment of

Table 13.7   Sample Recognition Summary Chart

	Daily	*Monthly/ Periodic*	*Periodic/Annual*
Customer focus	Quality awards that support customer needs	Periodic letters and awards by customers	Major customer events New customers
Broad Participation	Individual who contribute ideas or work on teams	Broader team results	For team and individual achievement
Process Improvement	Daily gains or accomplishments	Monthly gains from financials	Annual gains or accomplishments
Process management	Problems linked to process issues	Problems linked to process issues	Most improved process
Problem solving	Team-based problem-solving process and results	Steering committee monthly meeting	None currently exists
Visual measurements	Gains through visible means against visible metrics	None currently exists	None currently exists
Inspirational Leadership	None currently exists	Leadership behaviors or results that reflect leadership	Annual leadership awards

improvement goals. Financial recognition can be monetary in nature, or may be a system where prizes or items can be selected.

For example, I have implemented systems where awardees can select from a catalog of goods. One benefit of this is that a fixed amount of funds can be used to do more.

In addition, not assigning cash bonuses to specific behaviors avoids the problem that people then compare one award to another and can readily note differences. If people earn points for behaviors and then eventually buy something with the points, there is less chance of morale issues arising from one person getting more or less than another person for a similar act or behavior.

Sharing the Gains from Continuous Improvement

Bonus programs that reward groups of people for achieving goals or gains are a common feature linked to high-performing teams where everyone participates in the goals. These programs can be called different names and be designed in different ways. However, they generally contain a feature that financial gains to the organization are shared with those involved in the work. These programs have been shown to work as a motivational tool or incentive to achieve improvements. However, many of these same programs have problems that create unintended consequences that must be considered carefully before proceeding.

A feature of these programs that can be particularly helpful is educating employees about business decisions as they link to the payout of the financial sharing. However, the educational feature is only as strong as the effort to help employees work through financial considerations in detail and mentor them to a much higher level of understanding.

Beware of Disconnects

The first issue in terms of implementing a continuous improvement culture and rewards system is that typically, the original bonus programs or approaches will not be in alignment with the values related to these cultures. For example, a common reward structure in many organizations is to reward the highest levels of management the most, and many times, there are no bonus programs for the other employees. The theory behind these bonus structures is that the few at the top make the most important contributions and drive the results, so they should be awarded accordingly.

In contrast, a continuous improvement culture has a different view, that *all* people have a contribution to make and that success comes from everyone. Therefore, over the long haul, you need to align your rewards programs with the culture that exists.

That said, however, it is important to make changes to pay structures, after in-depth consideration to prevent missteps. It may still be better to live with an older program that disconnects from the culture than to quickly change compensation programs to ill-designed options. Pay can be a more powerful demotivator than motivator, so caution must be exercised to ensure the outcome is positive and not create more damage than good. In fact, motivation is such an important part of a continuous improvement culture that the next chapter is devoted to examining how Lean principles create a naturally motivated workplace.

CHAPTER 13 SUMMARY

KEY IDEAS

- Four core HR processes drive the majority of this department's efforts:
  1. Recruitment
  2. Training
  3. Performance management
  4. Rewards.

- Each core program contains several related processes that work together. For example, recruitment actually comprises recruiting, selecting, and on-boarding new employees.
- Training programs to support Lean principles are some of the most developed aspects of Lean HR so far. However, the HR department is often not involved in some of these training efforts.
- Performance management is one of the more controversial of the core HR processes in its effect on psychological safety and motivation. Give careful consideration to the approach taken and the impact on people.
- Recognition as part of the rewards program is generally under-utilized as a method to reinforce behaviors in people.

STRATEGIC QUESTIONS FOR HR

1. How well does your organization recognize behaviors to empha-size in the core HR processes?_____

_____

_____

_____

_____

2. How well do your current reward programs achieve desired results? _____
_____
_____
_____
_____
_____

3. Are there demotivating factors to your core HR processes? _____
_____
_____
_____
_____
_____

LEAN HR IMPLEMENTATION ACTIONS

1. Develop a plan for linking your HR processes to your business strategy and to effectively align them to achieve a strong culture, which may include features of continuous improvement:
   ■ List the elements of your four core HR processes now. _____
   _____
   _____
   _____
   _____
   _____
   _____

   ■ List the key elements of your business strategy. _____
   _____
   _____
   _____
   _____
   _____
   _____
   _____
   _____

   ■ Based on the lists, do you see links between the processes and your business strategy? _____

_____

_____

_____

_____

_____

_____

_____

■ For each process—recruitment, training, performance management, and rewards—list the elements that would link that process to your desired culture and business strategy. _____

_____

_____

_____

_____

_____

■ Compare the list of Lean principles with each of your core HR processes and list areas of opportunity that would suit your workplace. _____

_____

_____

_____

_____

_____

_____

■ For each element of your current processes, look for disconnects to Lean cultures that may need to be eliminated. _____

_____

_____

_____

_____

_____

_____

■ For each element of a process that you want to strengthen, develop actionable items that will implement that element. For example, if you want teamwork to be featured in each process to strengthen your culture, then the recruitment process might begin with team-based interviews, the training process would include team-oriented training, performance management would be adjusted to include an evaluation of each person's ability to work on teams or accomplishment through teamwork, and rewards might be changed to a team-based reward system. These changes could be implemented over several years._____

_____

_____

_____

_____

_____

2. Develop a one page outline that provides an overview of your four core HR processes and reflects what key elements are contained in all four processes. Put the HR processes across the top and the key elements you want in your programs down the left margin. Do you have any gaps or opportunities?

Chapter 14

A Five-Year Plan for Change

This book has provided some thoughts and ideas on how HR can support the implementation of a continuous improvement culture. The mandate to fully implement culture change is generally new, so organizations are hungry for answers as to how an organization actually pursues a culture change.

I encourage *you* to seek your own versions of these models and to apply them in ways that are natural to *your* organization. Continuous improvement cultures can deliver superior results over time, if the improved performance is based on cultural change, which means new norms for how people respond in your workplace, or normative behaviors or instinctive responses. Your plans to change your culture must be extensive and far reaching to allow for sufficient changes to previous ways of working. Change can be quite challenging.

Many of the concepts presented in this book were purposely repetitive to reinforce the fact that your messages should be *consistent*. The material applies the same seven Lean principles of *customer focus, broad participation, continuous improvement, process management, problem solving, visual measurement*, and *inspired leadership* to each aspect of HR programs and practices. (As shown in Table 1.1 in Chapter 1.) The repetition is what creates *alignment* of messages, which in turn builds enough momentum so that employees are clear about how they need to modify their behavior to new expectations. The process of changing the role of leadership to drive improvement is daunting, and it requires a tremendous amount of dedication to the cause.

The process of HR working as a partner in the organization's overall business strategy can begin with questioning or understanding what a leader is seeking to achieve in the next year (or some other period of time). Then, ask this same leader how he or she would like it if HR could do the following:

- Ensure that the people being hired are best able to achieve those results.
- Develop and conduct training so the leader can develop key behaviors in his or her people, to best achieve those results.
- Create accountability systems that the leader can use to work with people to best achieve those results.
- Create recognition systems to best support those results, which the leader(s) will handle but that HR will support.
- Support rewards programs that promote or reward the goals the leader wants to accomplish.
- Create celebrations that promote the behaviors to accomplish these goals.
- Support the measurement systems of the leader(s) to ensure people understand the goals.
- Surface issues that help improve results.
- Understand how the leader is held accountable and is actively supporting these same objectives.

If an HR professional could accomplish all of the above, leaders would consider that person to be an obvious value to them and an integral part of supporting their effort to align the human capital of the organization in a direction that supports the goals. Each HR practice needs to support an overarching goal of the leadership. Once aligned, HR can provide significant momentum, alignment, and support to achieving goals that may make all the difference in achieving them. Only through a partnership orientation can these efforts truly work.

How to Put Together a Five-Year Plan

Developing plans is primarily a partner activity, so the answer to this question cannot come from a book. The approach is grounded in the needs and priorities of the key functions HR support. The needs of *your* business or organization, with current pressures and challenges, will also drive the answer of where to start and what to do next. Look for openings where interest levels or current ideas match the items above. In addition, be prepared to present ideas and concepts as suggestions to meet strategic needs.

Also, update your five-year plan every year, to encompass and respond to changes in the environment. Progress with these efforts is the fundamental key to developing a stronger HR department, organizational culture, and finally, a more successful workforce.

Consider Management Roles and Maturity of Improvement Efforts

Sections III and IV presented an enormous amount of information about possible changes to make in the human resources area, so it's important to keep in mind that a critical error would be to take on too many changes at once. The timeframe for transforming the HR department is generally *a five-year plan*. Table 14.1 should give you an idea of how you can phase in your initial plans, in transitions, to improve how your organization optimizes people, while strengthening the skills of your HR staff members at the same time.

Moreover, the purpose of Table 14.1 is not to lay a precise roadmap that you *must* follow, but to alert you that you need to make a series of choices about which core HR program to put into effect, and in the sequence that will work best for *your organization*. Your choices involve not only which HR program to put into effect, but which *employee group* to address with the changes. Table 14.1 covers how to make changes for each core HR process against varying factors of employee groups and level of maturity for the improvement efforts. For example, the first row of column two for *senior-level management* shows selection activity of establishing a vision, followed by adding external resources for senior management selection, and ending with maintaining that approach to selection for the five-year plan. The second row for selection for *mid-level management* suggests revisions for new competencies, using team-based selection techniques, and ending with adding external resources. The third and final column for selection covers *nonmanagerial employees,* beginning with the status quo, moving to basic testing being added to the selection process, and ending with team-based selection processes.

Some organizations find that beginning with senior management makes the most sense because they can then provide the leadership needed for success. Other organizations find that beginning with nonmanagers will bring about enough momentum to sustain a change and bring others along

Table 14.1   Sample Time-Based Strategy for Implementing Lean HR

Lever	Senior Management	Mid-Level Management	Nonmanagers
Selection *Filters for the culture*	**First years:** Senior team lays out vision for selection	**First years:** Revise to new requirements for improvement competencies	**First years:** Status quo
	Middle years: Add external resources for senior-level selections	**Middle years:** Add team-based selection	**Middle years:** Add basic testing
	Final plan years: Maintain	**Final plan years:** Add external resources	**Final plan years** Team-based selection
Training and development *Build the culture*	**First years:** Individual coaching	**First years:** Lean tools	**First years:** Lean tools
	Middle years: Define with 360° results	**Middle years:** Lean-related objectives	**Middle years:** Culture support
	Final years: Continue	**Final years:** Use 360°	**Final years:** Cross-training
Performance management *Accountability*	**First years:** Based on results	**First years:** Based on objectives	**First years:** Status quo
	Middle years: Results and culture score	**Middle years:** Expectations related to improvement	**Middle years:** Add basic testing
	Final plan years: Maintain	**Final plan years:** Use 360° feedback	**Final plan years:** Team-based selection

Table 14.1   Sample Time-Based Strategy for Implementing Lean HR (Continued)

Lever	Senior Management	Mid-Level Management	Nonmanagers
Rewards *Not just results, needs to support the culture*	**First years:** Individual coaching	**First years** Status quo	**First years:** Status quo
	Middle years: Define with 360° results	**Middle years:** Revise base pay and bonus plans	**Middle years:** Revise base pay and bonus programs
	Final years: Gainsharing or employee stock option plan (ESOP)	**Final years:** Gainsharing or ESOP	**Final years:** Gainsharing or ESOP

later. And other organizations find that beginning with middle management as leadership for the majority of the people is critical to establishing a new foundation for daily work flows.

The five-year plan is not just a matter of the HR strategy and related time-frames, but it should also take into account the *maturity level of the improvement effort.* If your improvement effort is in a beginning stage, organizations will often focus on training first and build in accountability and reward systems later. If your improvement effort is mature (i.e., more than 10 years old) you might have a more comprehensive approach that targets more areas in a five-year timeframe to bring the HR systems up to speed with the changes that have already been happening. Again, there is not a generic answer to these issues, but they are factors to consider in laying out your plans.

CHAPTER 14 SUMMARY

KEY IDEAS

- Change happens over time. Organizations need to develop five-year plans to gain perspective about changes that are needed.
- In developing a five-year plan, consider the roles of management, the timing of your plan, and the maturity of the improvement effort to make decisions and which areas to change and in what manner.

STRATEGIC QUESTIONS FOR HR

1. What is the maturity level of your improvement effort and how would that affect your five-year plan?_____

_____

_____

_____

_____

_____

2. What changes are you currently considering in your HR programs, and would they compare to the other four core HR processes?_____

_____

_____

_____

_____

_____

_____

LEAN HR IMPLEMENTATION ACTIONS

A five-year action plan will differ for each organization and is a highly customized process. Following is a list of actions that you can review to discover which next steps are right for you.

Five-Year Action Plan for Lean Human Resources

1. Assess the waste of people's abilities with a root cause analysis of why people may not be optimized. _____

_____

_____

_____

_____

_____

2. Assess the effectiveness of the HR department to optimize people, including a root cause of any ineffectiveness. _____

_____

_____

_____

_____

_____

_____

3. If your organization already has begun improvement efforts, evaluate the effectiveness of those change efforts. How thoroughly has the change effort been designed and executed in terms of daily behaviors and attitudes? _____

_____

_____

_____

_____

_____

4. Consider a new vision for HR. What skills would be the first priorities to develop in the HR staff members to improve their ability to drive results? _____

_____

_____

_____

_____

_____

5. Assess the HR processes for areas that need improvement. Consider this an exercise that improves service to internal customers first._____

_____

_____

_____

_____

_____

6. Consider whether making people a strategic advantage on a new level would enhance the sales plan and change the course of your organization. _____

_____

_____

_____

_____

_____

_____

7. Describe the daily behaviors and attitudes that would enhance your organization's success. _____

_____

_____

_____

_____

_____

8. Create a list of values that best represents the culture that will advance the mission of your organization. How do those values create emotional connections or alignment for the people involved? _____

_____

_____

_____

_____

_____

9. Evaluate your policy handbook, communications vehicles, celebrations, and other practices for how they do or do not support strategic directions. _____

_____

_____

_____

_____

_____

10. Explore how you could use surveys to improve your culture, employee satisfaction, and the relationship with your customers.

_____

_____

_____

_____

_____

_____

11. Consider the competencies needed for leaders as well as all employees of your organization to achieve success. _____

_____

_____

_____

_____

_____

12. Improve and standardize the roles of leaders, or people who manage others, first to create a new vision for how managers support people so they will contribute more on a daily basis. ___

_____

_____

_____

_____

_____

13. Redesign each of your HR programs to meet strategic needs, and choose which program to excel at, while addressing the maturing of improvement efforts and the advantages to working with specific employee groups. _____

_____

_____

_____

_____

_____

14. Develop detailed plans on a regular basis that are designed to increase motivation levels among employees. _____

_____

_____

_____

_____

_____

ESPECIALLY FOR CEOs   VI

We end this book with a special section for CEOs. Much of this book has been written for HR professionals as a roadmap for developing an HR strategy and necessary changes to optimize your people and achieve a highly successful culture. However, your mindset, as a CEO, about the role of HR needs to change or you will miss these opportunities to stop wasting the talent of your people. Secondary to wasting talent and failing at culture changes, allowing HR to predominantly handle administrative or policy policing function is a waste of the HR department adding greater value that is critical to the organizational improved success.

Chapter 15 highlights an important benefit of implementing this book with your HR team to achieve the results you want in your workplace. While there are many implementable changes covered in the previous chapters, this chapter looks at how the common Lean principles naturally motivate people to achieve more by feeling positive about themselves and their work. Conversely, this chapter also invites you to consider how the absence of these common Lean principles is actually de-motivating to people and diminishes their morale and productivity.

Chapter 15

The Benefits of Motivating the Human Spirit

This book began by describing how human potential or people's abilities are wasted in the workplace. The discussion closes with a look at how optimizing people is increasingly powerful as a naturally motivating system of managing people's efforts. The motivational aspect of Lean principles provides even more reasons for integrating them into an HR strategy, including that continuous improvement cultures create more than immediate results.. Each principle is naturally motivating and inspires people to contribute more of themselves in the workplace. Each Lean cultural element has its unique motivational aspect, which is a fraction of how they work together to create energy, enthusiasm, and the motivational power to accomplish tasks in far less time and with far better results. The principles build off of each other to create ever greater amounts of energy and enthusiasm. Each factor combines with the other elements to generate energy and momentum.

The importance of understanding the motivational elements of Lean is the benefit that can be channeled for improved results. Equally true is that failing to integrate sound principles for people management certainly causes results to suffer. This chapter describes how each of the seven common Lean principles creates motivation and can be intentionally implemented through a range of practices. This chapter ends with highlighting the mutual benefits that these factors bring to employees, customers, and the shareholders, better referred to as a *triple win*. We begin with the seven motivational factors below:

1. *Meaning* from customer focus
2. *Accomplishment* from continual improvement
3. *Engagement* from participation
4. *Personal* value from process management
5. *Satisfaction* from teamwork and problem solving
6. *Achievement* from measuring visible results
7. *Ownership* from personal leadership

> If a Lean culture is naturally motivating, much of traditional business cultures are clearly demotivating.

1. **Motivating people by bringing a sense of meaning to their work.**
   Strengthening how employees connect with their customers motivates people by bringing meaning to their work. A range of opportunities exists for creating mechanisms and communications that help employees make a real connection to customers. Employees like to be more aware of how their work links to the customer's needs in a way that is clear and tangible. Here are a few ways you can heighten the motivation from this principle:
   - Put customer logos out in visible locations.
   - Provide customer information to employees that link their work to the importance of customer needs.
   - Provide information on customers' likes, dislikes, and requirements.
   - Invite customers into the workplace to speak to employees about what is important to them and their organization's mission.

2. **Motivating people by giving them a sense of accomplishment.**
   Continuous improvement is motivational in the sense of accomplishment that comes from making gains. Here are a few ways you can increase accomplishment:
   - Teach people what preventable defects means.
   - Teach people how to create sustainable processes.
   - Celebrate gains on a regular basis.
   - Look for ways that improvement efforts create successful feelings.

3. **Motivating people by engaging them.** When people share their ideas, they usually find it rewarding, especially when they see their ideas being considered (even if their ideas are not implemented). Engagement from participation is a significant opportunity for companies to provide people with a sense of contribution, value, and respect by seeking their opinions and suggestions. Here are some suggestions on how to engage employees:

   ■ Actively seek employees' opinions on a wide variety of topics.
   ■ Whenever possible, seek input on decisions that affect employees.
   ■ Publicly recognize contributions by employees that are acted on.
   ■ Train supervisors in how to engage employees.
   ■ Protect employees from any type of abusive behavior or punitive measures that hurt engagement.

4. **Motivating people by removing waste in the work they do.** Process management brings to light the waste in processes. People often experience the waste in processes as demotivating: doing things twice, getting the wrong goods in their area, or passing along defective items. Conversely, people are pleased to identify these wastes and see them removed as a way to create more value to their time and efforts. Following are a few ways to increase motivation in the area of process management:

   ■ Teach people about process management and how to identify waste in work processes.
   ■ Celebrate waste removal from processes.
   ■ Be careful not to link messages or movements to reduce the number of people in the workplace with process-improvement activities.
   ■ Have people share stories of waste removal in your organization's newsletter.
   ■ Take people to other organizations that have removed waste to energize them about possibilities in their own workplaces.

5. **Motivating people by providing satisfaction from teamwork and problem solving.** Team-based problem solving allows people to work with others to solve problems. Because the process is done in teams, people learn more about others and the challenge others face in their work. This team learning allows people to appreciate

others and to feel better understood. Here are a few ways to foster this satisfaction:

- Recognize team efforts.
- Especially highlight how people came to understand each other better and hence enjoy their days more.

6. **Motivating people by recognizing personal achievement.** The use of visible results creates an environment of achievement by making results easy for employees to understand and monitor, on a daily, if not hourly, basis. Achievement and "making your numbers" is somewhat like a game to people, and it's no fun to play a game if you can't even tell who is winning! Therefore, people use visible metrics as reference points that they can then use to measure their progress. As they see achievement of new goals or measures, they feel encouraged by the achievement and hence are motivated. The opportunity is for companies to ensure all key metrics are visibly located for employees to see. Here are a few ways:

- Post results where others can see them.
- Have people participate in creating visual measurements.
- Conduct training on visual measurements.
- Have people benchmark other organizations that utilize visual measurements to create success.

7. **Motivating people by fostering a sense of ownership.** Leadership and teaching others to lead creates an immense amount of motivation. People are hungry to contribute more of themselves and show personal leadership. Improvement efforts create an opportunity to motivate people by taking leadership in following through on problems, suggestions, issues, customer concerns, etc. At the risk of using the over-used term *empowerment*, the visionary leadership of a Lean organization is devoted to empowering others. Empowering others is motivating. In Lean organizations, many people get a chance to show leadership, instead of only the few "in charge." Here are a few ways to foster a sense of ownership:

- Debrief leaders when they empower others.
- Recognize managers who actively empower others.
- Teach or train managers in the skills linked to empowerment.
- Hold managers accountable for empowering others.

Optimizing Human Potential and Motivation Creates a Triple Win

Using the motivational factors of Lean creates a triple win by achieving:

1. More satisfied customers, which can lead to increased revenues and improved pricing levels.
2. More satisfied employees, which can lead to improved operations and revenue-generating results.
3. More satisfied ownership from the improved revenues and profitability levels from the first two groups.

Let's look at each of these in a bit more detail.

Resulting Customer Benefits

Customers absolutely are aware of more engaged employees. A culture or organization that is highly motivated is easily seen by customers in their interactions across any and all of the departments within the organization. Does the customer service department seem really interested in their problem, or is someone merely following a manual? Is each request or need met with enthusiasm and interest? Is the customer given suggestions for how to get what they need or reasons why they can't get their needs met? In an organization with broader leadership, the customer likely finds people at all levels stepping into leadership to solve issues instead of merely sending a problem up to a manager to resolve.

Resulting Employee Benefits

The benefits of creating a highly motivated work force is that an organization can recruit and retain better talent, experience minimal turnover, and create greater employee satisfaction. More highly qualified talent will seek employment in organizations with strong cultures. Turnover is often the result of demotivated employees who need some type of attention to meet their needs. Much of what helps motivate employees also drives the organizational benefits as well.

Resulting Organizational Benefits

The benefits to the company of having a highly motivated workforce are greater profits from heightened revenue and decreased costs from removing wastes, as well as the benefits of having improved relations with customers and employees. The increased profits can be significant, which is why so much focus has been placed on Lean methodologies. Improved relations with employees and customers drive both measurable and general benefits to an organization.

CHAPTER 15 SUMMARY

KEY IDEAS

- Lean principles are naturally motivating.
- Workplaces are often demotivating, which tends to reduce or restrict productivity.
- Creating a highly motivated successful workforce creates a triple win for the customer, the employee, and the organization as a whole.

STRATEGIC QUESTIONS FOR THE CEO

1. If Lean principles are motivating, then how might your current practices be demotivating?
2. What would be the benefit of increasing the motivation levels in your organization?

LEAN HR IMPLEMENTATION ACTIONS FOR THE CEO

1. Develop ideas for the Lean principles below to optimize the motivating feature in a multitude of ways. *Keep in mind that each idea has the power to generate additional motivation when in turn increases the employee morale and productivity of your workforce.*

   My ideas for how my organization can implement changes to:

- Increase the meaning people get from connecting to our customers:

- Increase the sense of accomplishment people get from achieving continual gains:

- Increase the sense of people's engagement from greater participation in your workplace:

- Increase people's sense of personal value from understanding their role in our total business processes and that we improve them for their benefit (as well as our customers):

- Increase the sense of satisfaction people get from working together to solve problems and ensuring the problems don't repeat:

- Increase the sense of achievement from people get from being able to see the results of their work efforts through the visual display of their results:

- Increase the sense of ownership people possess when they are invited to lead, have opportunities to lead and are rewarded for coaching others to lead:

2. Develop ideas for the Lean principles below to minimize possible de-motivating features in your work environment through specific implementation ideas. *Again, keep in mind that each idea your organization implements has the power to generate additional motivation to increase morale and productivity.*
   My ideas for making changes to remove de-motivating conditions that cause our people to feel:

- Their work has little meaning or importance by lacking a tangible connection to our external customers:

- A sense of failure or complacency by not experiencing continual gains:

- Disengaged because their opinions are not sought (hence not valued) and they are not invited to participate in changes that effect them:

- Isolated and that their work as filled with unsolved problems:

- A sense of failure (and hurt) when they are blamed or personally criticized when things go wrong:

- They don't make a difference because they have no measure of their work's success:

- Minimize the loss of ownership by only a few being given opportunities to lead:

Index

The Author

Cheryl Jekiel brings a tremendous passion for continuous improvement in her commitment to building Lean HR as a recognized field of work. Ms. Jekiel has over 20 years of manufacturing experience, including currently working as the vice president of Human Resources for Flying Food Group, headquartered in Chicago, IL. Previously, Ms. Jekiel worked for a Chicago food manufacturer as the director of Human Resources and completed her employment by serving for five years as the Chief Operating Officer.

Ms. Jekiel has developed an expertise in Lean manufacturing in over 20 years of practice, with a particular focus on Lean cultures. Ms. Jekiel has made countless significant improvements in reducing operating costs and leveraging a "Lean culture" to obtain new business. Her Lean experience has been greatly enhanced with her active involvement with the Association of Manufacturing Excellence (AME), which has included board roles for the National board as well as a Regional Midwest Board.